Cupcake Fun!

Over 150 Cupcake And Treat Designs For Every Occasion

Dear Friend,

Grown-ups have discovered what kids have always known—cupcakes are the perfect party dessert. The birthday favorite we all grew up with is creating great excitement at a wide variety of events, from holiday parties to wedding receptions. Young or old, at any celebration, it's always a thrill to be served a treat that is decorated just for you.

Cupcake Fun! is the ideal place to discover the excitement of cupcakes. In this collection, Wilton presents cupcakes like none you have ever seen. The party people on our cover set the tone perfectly. Baked and served in our Silly-Feet! footed silicone cups, they are easy-to-make treats that are irresistible for party-goers of all ages. These cupcakes actually stand up to welcome guests to the party fun.

In *Cupcake Fun!*, even traditional round cupcakes are transformed into captivating new shapes. Here, a cupcake can become anything from a cup of coffee to a flying saucer. You can build a baby bassinette with a single cupcake on a candy platform, or arrange an entire batch on a stand to form a festive ski slope centerpiece for the holidays. And round cupcakes are just the start—you'll see terrific designs made in our heart, diamond and square cups as well.

Planning your celebration is easy using the exciting theme ideas in *Cupcake Fun!* From princess carriages, castles and crowns for a girl's birthday to pacifiers and diaper pins for the baby shower, the book is organized around theme designs that look great together. With so many coordinated themes to choose from, it's easy to add variety to the party and serve each guest something special.

Flavor is also a big part of the excitement in *Cupcake Fun!* Our recipe section is packed with delicious surprises like Key Lime Cupcakes, Mocha Icing and Praline Filling. With the convenient Flavor Combinations Chart, it's easy to create cupcakes that taste as great as they look. For even more great recipes and ideas, check the ultimate cupcake website, www.cupcakefun.com.

It's time to start planning your cupcake celebration with *Cupcake Fun!*. Use the sensational ideas inside, along with easy instructions and our exclusive cupcake products to create an event to delight every guest.

Vince Naccarato

Vince Naccarato
Chairman and CEO
Wilton Industries, Inc.

Credits

Creative Director
Daniel Masini

Art Director/Cake Designer
Steve Rocco

Decorating Room Supervisor
Mary Gavenda

Senior Cake Decorator
Susan Matusiak

Cake Decorators
Jenny Jurewicz • Diane Knowlton
Mark Malak • Tracey Wurzinger
Judy Wysocki • Debbie Friedman

Editor/Writer
Jeff Shankman

Writers
Mary Enochs
Marita Seiler

Copy Editor
Jane Mikis

Production Manager
Challis Yeager

Associate Production Manager
Mary Stahulak

Graphic Design/Production
Marek/Janci Design
Courtney Kieras

Photography
Dale DeBolt
Peter Rossi—PDR Productions
Black Box

Photo Stylist
Carey Thornton

Creative Services Assistant
Sharon Gaeta

Product Manager
Tina Celeste

IN U.S.A.
Wilton Industries, Inc.
2240 West 75th Street
Woodridge, IL 60517
www.wilton.com
Retail Customer Orders:
Phone: 800-794-5866 • Fax: 888-824-9520
Online: www.wilton.com
Class Locations:
Phone: 800-942-8881
Online: www.wilton.com/classes

IN CANADA
Wilton Industries, Canada, Ltd.
98 Carrier Drive
Etobicoke, Ontario M9W5R1 Canada
Retail Customer Orders:
Phone: 416-679-0798
Class Locations:
Phone: 416-679-0790, ext. 200
E-mail: classprograms@wilton.ca

¡SE HABLA ESPAÑOL!
Para mas informacion,
marque 800-436-5778

Table of Contents

64

10

74

89

96

BIRTHDAYS

All You Could Wish For!

Kids never cared about how convenient cupcakes were for Mom. They only knew that cupcakes were a lot more fun to eat than a big birthday cake. No forks, no plates—you could just grab one and start munching. Best of all, every kid at the party had his own complete treat.

Today, it's grown-ups who have discovered the fun side of cupcakes. This section is the perfect place to find great new ways to serve, like the stand-up party people here, baked in our Silly-Feet! Silicone cups. See cupcakes shaped like BBQ grills or built into a giant ferris wheel. Or make them elegant with pretty icing roses and fondant bouquets. Cupcakes are ready for the spotlight!

Shown: *Stand Up and Cheer!*; instructions, p. 94 and *The Wishmakers*; instructions, p. 10.

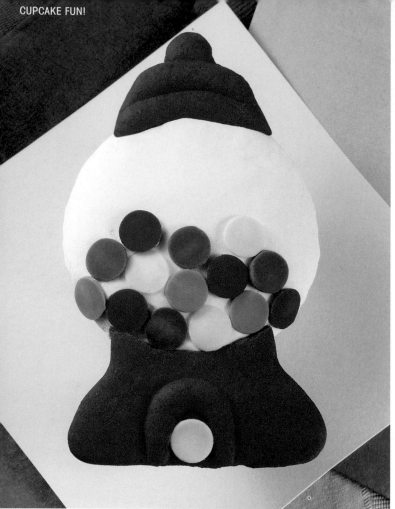

‹ Have Fun, By Gum!

PANS: Jumbo Muffin; Cookie Sheet; Cooling Grid
COLOR: Red-Red
FONDANT: Primary Colors Fondant Multi Pack; Round Cut-Outs™; Rolling Pin; Roll & Cut Mat
RECIPES: Buttercream Icing, p. 101; Roll-Out Cookie, p. 103
ALSO: White Jumbo Baking Cups; 101 Cookie Cutters Set; 4 in. Lollipop Sticks; Cake Board; Spatula; waxed paper

See "Wilton Products", p. 118-127 for most Wilton items used in this project.

In advance: Roll out fondant colors 1/8 in. thick. Cut gumballs using smallest Cut-Out. Set aside on waxed paper-covered board. **Also:** Tint cookie dough red. Roll out and cut cookie using bell cutter from set; cut off clapper. Cut cookie 2 in. from bottom for base of machine; use remainder for top of machine. Roll two 3/8 in. logs of dough for top cookie and one for machine opening; position. Using large round cookie cutter from set, cut curve in top and bottom cookies to conform to cupcake. Bake and cool cookies. Cut lollipop sticks to 3 in.; attach to back of cookies, leaving 1 1/2 in. extended.

Ice cupcakes smooth. Insert cookies in cupcakes. Position fondant gumballs.

Learning the Basics ›

PAN: Mini Loaf
TIPS: 4, 6, 9, 47
COLORS:* Black, Brown, Red-Red
FONDANT: Primary Colors Fondant Multi Pack; Alphabet/Number Cut-Outs™; Rolling Pin; Roll & Cut Mat
RECIPE: Buttercream Icing, p. 101
ALSO: Gold Foil Petite Loaf Cups; Spatula; Cake Board; waxed paper

See "Wilton Products", p. 118-127 for most Wilton items used in this project.

Roll out fondant colors 1/8 in. thick; cut letters and numbers using Cut-Outs. Set aside on waxed paper-covered board. Ice mini loaf cake smooth in black. For border, pipe tip 47 smooth side up. For ledge, pipe tip 9 band at bottom. Pipe tip 4 outline chalk. Pipe tip 6 outline eraser; flatten with spatula to make square shape. Position letters and numbers.

* Combine Brown with Red-Red for brown shown.

Twinkling Stars

PANS: Standard Muffin; Cookie Sheet; Cooling Grid

TIP: 2

COLORS: Lemon Yellow, Violet, Rose, Royal Blue

RECIPES: Buttercream, Color Flow Icings, p. 101; Roll-Out Cookie, p. 103

ALSO: Cupcakes 'N More® Dessert Stand (holds 13); Sparkling Sugars in Yellow, Violet, Pink and Blue; Color Mist™ in Yellow, Violet, Pink and Blue; White Standard Baking Cups; Nesting Stars Metal Cutter Set; Rolling Pin; Color Flow Mix; Parchment Triangles; Spatula

See "Wilton Products", p. 118-127 for most Wilton items used in this project.

In advance: Roll out dough. Cut cookies using smallest star cutter; bake and cool. Outline with tip 2 using tinted full-strength color flow in parchment bag; flow in with thinned color flow. Let set 10 minutes, then sprinkle with matching color sugar; let dry.

Spatula ice cupcakes in buttercream. Spray with Color Mist; sprinkle with matching sugar. Insert cookie; support with icing if needed. Position cupcakes on stand.

< Let Them Fly!

PAN:	Standard Muffin
TIP:	3
COLORS:	Red-Red, Royal Blue, Lemon Yellow
RECIPE:	Buttercream Icing, p. 101
ALSO:	White Standard Baking Cups; Spatula; curling ribbon

See "Wilton Products", p. 118-127 for most Wilton items used in this project.

Ice cupcakes smooth. Pipe tip 3 outline highlight. Add tip 3 spiral balloon neck on edge. Cut ribbon, curl and insert into balloon neck.

Fun for One >

PANS:	Standard Muffin; Cookie Sheet; Cooling Grid
TIPS:	3, 4, 6
COLORS:*	Lemon Yellow, Golden Yellow, Rose, Leaf Green, Violet
RECIPES:	Buttercream, Royal Icings, p. 101; Roll-Out Cookie, p. 103
ALSO:	Square Cut-Outs™; Assorted Celebration Candles; Party Time Standard Baking Cups; Meringue Powder; Rolling Pin; Spatula; 4 in. Lollipop Sticks; waxed paper

See "Wilton Products", p. 118-127 for most Wilton items used in this project.

In advance: Tint cookie dough yellow. Roll out and cut cookies in birthday cake shape using medium square Cut-Out; bake and cool. Position cookies on waxed paper. Using royal icing, pipe tip 6 swirls to create iced cake top; pipe tip 3 scallop garland with tip 4 dots at scallop points; let set. Trim lollipop stick to 2 1/2 in. Attach candle and stick to back of cookie; let set.

Ice cupcakes smooth in buttercream; insert cookie. Pipe tip 6 ball bottom border on cookie in buttercream.

* Combine Violet with Rose for violet shown. Combine Lemon Yellow with Golden Yellow for yellow shown.

‹ Snack-in-the-Box

PAN: Cookie Sheet
TIPS: 5, 32
COLORS: Red-Red, Royal Blue, Lemon Yellow
FONDANT: White Ready-To-Use Rolled Fondant, Rolling Pin, Roll & Cut Mat
RECIPE: Buttercream Icing, p. 101
ALSO: Square Silicone Baking Cups; 4 in. Lollipop Sticks; Small Derby Clowns Set; Spatula; ruler, pizza cutter, scissors

See "Wilton Products", p. 118-127 for most Wilton items used in this project.

Tint portions of fondant to match silicone cups. Roll out fondant 1/8 in. thick; cut a 2^{1}/$_{2}$ in. square for box lid. Let dry for 24 to 48 hours.

Bake and cool cupcakes in silicone cups supported by cooling grid. Ice cupcakes smooth. Figure pipe clown (p. 110) using tips 32 and 5.

Hats Incredible! ›

PAN: Standard Muffin
TIPS: 3, 8, 13
COLORS:* Lemon Yellow, Golden Yellow, Violet, Rose, Leaf Green
RECIPE: Buttercream Icing, p. 101
ALSO: Party Time Standard Baking Cups; Spatula; sugar ice cream cones, scissors

See "Wilton Products", p. 118-127 for most Wilton items used in this project.

Cut cones to 3 in. high by gently cutting along open end with scissors. Ice smooth. Pipe tip 3 dots or tip 8 stripes on cones. Position in center of cupcake. Pipe tip 13 pull-out stars around base and for pompom on cone.

* Combine Lemon Yellow with Golden Yellow for yellow shown.

< The Wishmakers

PAN: Cookie Sheet
TIP: 1M (2110)
COLORS: Kelly Green, Rose, Lemon Yellow
FONDANT: White Ready-To-Use Rolled Fondant; Fondant Ribbon Cutter/Embosser; Rolling Pin; Roll & Cut Mat
RECIPE: Buttercream Icing, p. 101
ALSO: Pastel Silicone Baking Cups; Smiley Flames Chunky Candles; Spatula; candy-coated chocolate dots

See "Wilton Products", p. 118-127 for most Wilton items used in this project.

Bake and cool cupcakes in silicone cups supported by cookie sheet. Pipe tip 1M swirl on cupcake tops. Tint portions of fondant to match cups. Roll out $1/8$ in. thick. Using straight-edge wheels from Cutter/Embosser, cut five $1/4$ x 2 in. strips for each cupcake. Twist strip slightly; attach to cupcake with icing, in a garland formation. Position chocolate dots. Insert candle.

Wrapped Up Bright! >

PAN: Cookie Sheet
RECIPE: Buttercream Icing, p. 101
ALSO: Square Silicone Baking Cups; Stars, Confetti and Nonpareils Jumbo Sprinkle Decorations; Spatula; spice drops, uncooked spaghetti, granulated sugar, waxed paper

See "Wilton Products", p. 118-127 for most Wilton items used in this project.

Bake and cool cupcakes in silicone cups supported by cookie sheet; ice smooth. Roll out spice drops on waxed paper sprinkled with sugar. Cut ribbon strips $3/8$ x $2 1/2$ in. long; attach with icing. For bow, cut 2 teardrop shapes, $1 1/4$ in. long; attach. For knot, cut spice drop horizontally in half; attach top half. Insert spaghetti in cupcake top to support bow; attach bow with icing. Position sprinkles, cutting to fit as needed.

‹Silly-Feet Treats!

PANS: Cookie Sheet

TIPS: 1A, 3, 12, 21

COLORS:* Copper (skin tone), Black, Orange, Red-Red, Royal Blue, Yellow, Violet, Rose

RECIPES: Buttercream, Royal Icings, p. 101

ALSO: Hands Pattern, p. 114; Silly-Feet Silicone Baking Cups; Jumbo Sprinkle Decorations in Diamonds, Stars and Confetti; Sour Cherry Balls Sprinkle Decorations; 4 in. Lollipop Sticks; Rolling Pin; Meringue Powder; Spatula; sugar ice cream cones, granulated sugar, cornstarch, waxed paper, yellow spice drops, scissors

See "Wilton Products", p. 118-127 for most Wilton items used in this project.

In advance: Make hats. Cut cones to 1¹/₂ in. high by gently cutting along open end with scissors. Ice smooth and decorate using royal icing. Attach sprinkles. Add tip 3 pull-out pompom. Let dry.

Bake and cool cupcakes in silicone cups supported by cookie sheet. Cover cupcake tops with tip 1A mound. Smooth with spatula to create rounded head. For arms, cut sticks to 3 in. long. Insert stick 2¹/₂ in. into bag fitted with tip 21; squeeze as you pull out stick to pipe arms. Insert arms into cupcake. For hands, roll out spice drops on waxed paper sprinkled with sugar; using pattern, cut hands with scissors. Attach hands to arms with royal icing. Pipe tip 3 dot or outline eyes, pupils and pipe-in mouth. Position hat on head; pipe tip 3 pull-out fringe brim. Pipe tip 12 dot cheeks (pat smooth with finger dipped in cornstarch). Position sour cherry nose.

*Combine Violet with Rose for violet shown. Combine Orange with Red-Red for orange shown.

A Clown's Never Down ›

PANS: Cookie Sheet; Cooling Grid

TIPS: 3, 12, 47, 102

COLORS:* Royal Blue, Copper (skin tone), Rose, Black, Lemon Yellow

RECIPES: Buttercream, Royal Icings, p. 101; Roll-Out Cookie, p. 103

ALSO: Hands Pattern, p. 114; Silly-Feet Silicone Baking Cups; Meringue Powder; 101 Cookie Cutters Set; 6 in. Lollipop Sticks; Rolling Pin; Spatula; mini and standard candy-coated chocolate dots, green fruit slices, spice drops, granulated sugar, scissors, waxed paper, ruler

See "Wilton Products", p. 118-127 for most Wilton items used in this project.

In advance: Make cookie heads. Tint dough copper; roll out. Cut heads using smallest round cutter from set; bake and cool. Cut sticks in half; attach to cookies with royal icing. Let set. Decorate heads with royal icing. Roll out purple and orange spice drops on waxed paper sprinkled with sugar; cut into ⁵/₈ x 1 in. triangles. Cut slits in orange drops for hair. Attach pieces with icing. Pipe tip 102 ruffle hat band. Add tip 3 pull-out pompom. Pipe tip 3 string mouth, dot eyes and cheeks (flatten slightly). Attach mini chocolate nose.

Bake and cool cupcakes in silicone cups supported by cookie sheet. Ice cupcakes smooth in buttercream, mounding to form rounded body. Pipe tip 47 smooth side up band suspenders. Insert head. For arms, cut sticks to 2¹/₂ in. Roll out green fruit slice; cut hands using pattern. Insert sticks ³/₈ in. deep into hands; insert other end in bag fitted with tip 12; squeeze as you pull out stick to pipe arms. Insert arms in body. Position standard size chocolate buttons.

This Spells Fun!

PANS: Cookie Sheet; Cooling Grid

COLORS: Leaf Green, Orange, Violet, Lemon Yellow, Rose, Royal Blue

RECIPES: Buttercream Icing, p. 101; Roll-Out Cookie, p. 103

ALSO: Pastel Silicone Baking Cups (2 pks.); Colored Sugars in Light Green, Orange, Lavender, Yellow, Pink, Blue; White Candy Melts®†; 101 Cookie Cutters Set; 4 in. Lollipop Sticks; Rolling Pin; Spatula

See "Wilton Products", p. 118-127 for most Wilton items used in this project.

Divide cookie dough in 6 portions; tint blue, rose, yellow, green, orange and violet. Roll out and cut message using alphabet cutters from set. Sprinkle cookies with matching colored sugars; bake and cool. Cut lollipop sticks in lengths of 2 1/2 to 3 in.; attach to cookie backs using melted candy, leaving 1 1/2 in. extended at bottom. Let set.

Bake and cool cupcakes in silicone cups supported by cookie sheet. Ice smooth; sprinkle with colored sugars to match cookies. Insert cookies in cupcakes.

‹ Crayon Creations

PAN: 10¹/₂ x 15¹/₂ in. Jelly Roll

TIP: 2

COLORS: Royal Blue, Red, Orange, Black

FONDANT: White Ready-To-Use Rolled Fondant; Rolling Pin; Roll & Cut Mat; Oval Cut-Outs™; Fondant Ribbon Cutter/Embosser; Brush Set

RECIPES: Buttercream Icing, p. 101; Jelly Roll Yellow Sponge Cake, p. 103

ALSO: Parchment Paper; large spice drops, vegetable oil pan spray, plastic wrap

See "Wilton Products", p. 118-127 for most Wilton items used in this project.

In advance: Bake and cool jelly roll cake following instructions. Unmold and fill with desired filling. Reroll and wrap in plastic wrap; freeze.

Cut thawed cake into 3 in. lengths. Tint portions of fondant light and dark blue, light and dark red, light and dark orange and black. Roll out all fondant ¹/₈ in. thick. Cover cakes with light blue, red or orange; trim ends to fit and smooth with fingers. Cover large spice drops with dark blue, red or orange; shape into crayon tip, using additional fondant for dimension. Smooth with fingers. Using medium Cut-Out, cut center oval in black; attach with damp brush. Print tip 2 color name. Using Cutter/ Embosser, cut ¹/₄ in. wide strips in black for borders; attach with damp brush. Attach crayon tip to cake with damp brush. For tip base, cut a 3 x ³/₈ in. wide strip in matching color; attach with damp brush.

Lucky Number ›

PAN: Cookie Sheet

TIP: 2

COLORS: Orange, Red-Red, Royal Blue, Kelly Green

CANDY: White Candy Melts®†; Numerals Candy Mold; Primary Candy Color Set

RECIPE: Buttercream Icing, p. 101

ALSO: Pastel Silicone Baking Cups; Spatula

See "Wilton Products", p. 118-127 for most Wilton items used in this project.

In advance: Make candy number (any age will work). Tint melted candy using candy colors; mold following mold package directions, filling ¹/₄ in. deep. Refrigerate until firm; unmold.

Bake and cool cupcakes in silicone cups supported by cookie sheet. Ice smooth. Position number. Print tip 2 message.

† Brand confectionery coating.

<King-Size Surprise!

PANS:	King-Size Muffin; Cooling Grid
TIPS:	3, 7, 9, 21
COLORS:	Leaf Green, Royal Blue, Lemon Yellow, Golden Yellow, Violet, Rose
RECIPES:	Buttercream, Quick-Pour Fondant Icings, p. 101
ALSO:	Smiley Flames Chunky Candles; Cake Board; Fanci-Foil Wrap; Cake Release; Pastry Brush; candy-coated chocolate dots, ruler, waxed paper, toothpicks

See "Wilton Products", p. 118-127 for most Wilton items used in this project.

Brush pan cavities with Cake Release; bake and cool cupcakes without baking cups. Trim cupcake tops level; lightly ice in buttercream. Turn over and cover cakes with poured fondant icing (p. 106); let dry. Position cupcakes on foil-covered boards cut to fit. Divide cakes in 6ths; measure and mark 2 in. from bottom. In buttercream, using tip 3 for all, pipe rose drop strings 1/4 in. deep, yellow zigzags 1/2 in. deep and blue drop strings 1 in. deep. Attach chocolate dots at string points. Pipe tip 7 top and tip 9 bottom ball borders. Pipe tip 21 rosette candleholder on cupcake top; insert candle.

Soft-Serve Swirl >

PAN:	King-Size Muffin
TIP:	1M (2110)
RECIPE:	Buttercream Icing, p. 101
ALSO:	White King-Size Baking Cups; Jumbo Nonpareils Sprinkle Decorations; Sour Cherry Balls Sprinkle Decorations; stick candy

See "Wilton Products", p. 118-127 for most Wilton items used in this project.

Pipe tip 1M swirl on cupcake tops. Sprinkle with nonpareils. Position cherry sprinkle; insert stick candy.

‹ Cool & Creamy

PAN: Cookie Sheet

TIP: 1M (2110)

RECIPE: Wilton Gelatin Treats, p. 102

ALSO: Pastel Silicone Baking Cups; Sour Cherry Balls Sprinkle Decorations; Vanilla Whipped Icing Mix, gelatin mix in blueberry, lime, strawberry, orange and lemon flavors (two 3 oz. pks. make 6-8 desserts), non-stick vegetable pan spray

See "Wilton Products", p. 118-127 for most Wilton items used in this project.

Spray baking cups with pan spray. Mold Gelatin Treats in silicone cups placed on cookie sheet; refrigerate until firm; unmold. Top all treats with a tip 1M swirl in whipped icing. Position cherry sprinkle.

Small Wonders ›

PAN: Mini Muffin

TIP: 12

COLORS: Lemon Yellow, Rose, Kelly Green, Royal Blue

RECIPE: Buttercream Icing, p. 101

ALSO: White Mini Baking Cups; Cupcakes 'N More® Mini Dessert Stand (holds 24); Colored Sugars in Yellow, Pink, Blue, Green

See "Wilton Products", p. 118-127 for most Wilton items used in this project.

Pipe tip 12 swirl on mini cupcake tops; sprinkle with matching colored sugar. Position on stand.

< Sundae Fun

PAN: Standard Muffin
TIP: 21
ALSO: White Standard Baking Cups; Flowerful Medley Sprinkle
Decorations; sundae glasses, ice cream, fudge sauce,
whipping cream, maraschino cherries

See "Wilton Products", p. 118-127 for most Wilton items used in this project.

Position cupcakes in sundae glass. Top with a scoop of ice cream
and cover with fudge sauce. Pipe a tip 21 swirl of whipped
cream; position cherry. Top with confetti sprinkles.

Cherry on Top >

PANS: Cookie Sheet; Cooling Grid; Non-Stick Jelly Roll
TIP: 1M (2110)
RECIPES: Buttercream Icing, p. 101; favorite crisped rice
cereal treats
ALSO: Pastel Silicone Baking Cups; Yellow Candy Melts®†;
Round Cut-Outs™; Rainbow Jimmies Sprinkle
Decorations; stick candy, mini candy-coated chocolate
dots, maraschino cherries with stems

See "Wilton Products", p. 118-127 for most Wilton items used in this project.

In advance: Make candy platform top and bottom for each treat.
Place large round Cut-Out on non-stick pan; fill 1/8 in. deep for
top with melted candy. Refrigerate until firm; repeat for bottom
piece, making it 1/4 in. deep. Trim stick candy to 3 in.; attach
to underside of platform top with melted candy. Let set. **Also:**
Prepare cereal treats. Press into jelly roll pan, 1/2 in. thick. Cut
treats using medium Cut-Out; cut a hole in center to fit stick
candy. Position on cooling grid over cookie sheet and cover
with melted candy; refrigerate until firm. Attach cereal treat to
platform bottom with melted candy; attach mini chocolate dots.
Insert stick candy in cereal treat; secure with melted candy.
Attach platform top to stick candy with melted candy. Let set.

Bake and cool cupcakes in silicone cups supported by cookie
sheet. Cover cupcakes with tip 1M swirl; sprinkle with jimmies.
Position cherry, then position cupcake on platform.

Candy Shop Surprise

PANS: Standard Muffin; Cookie Sheet; Cooling Grid
TIP: 1M (2110)
CANDY: White Candy Melts®† (3 pks. make 15 to 18 cupcakes); Primary, Garden Candy Color Sets
RECIPE: Buttercream Icing, p. 101
ALSO: Sour Cherry Balls Sprinkle Decorations; Cake Release; Parchment Triangles; Pastry Brush; scissors

See "Wilton Products", p. 118-127 for most Wilton items used in this project.

Brush pan cavities with Cake Release. Bake and cool cupcakes without baking cups. Divide 2 pks. melted candy in thirds; tint portions light violet, yellow and light pink using candy colors. Place cupcakes upside down on cooling grid over cookie sheet; cover with melted candy (p. 106). Let set; repeat if needed to coat completely. Divide remaining pk. melted candy in 5ths; tint portions dark pink, green, dark violet, orange and blue using candy colors. Using melted candy in cut parchment bag, pipe stripes, swirls and dots on sides of cupcakes. Pipe tip 1M swirl in buttercream on cupcake tops; position sprinkle.

† Brand confectionery coating.

‹ A Snack with Sizzle

PANS:	Mini Ball; Cooling Grid
CANDY:	Candy Melts®† in Red and White; Primary, Garden Candy Color Sets*
RECIPE:	Candy Clay, p. 102
ALSO:	8 in. Cookie Treat Sticks; Fanci-Foil Wrap; Rolling Pin; twist-up glue stick, waxed paper, paring knife

See "Wilton Products", p. 118-127 for most Wilton items used in this project.

For each treat, tint 1 oz. white candy (approximately 10 wafers) black using candy color. With remaining white candy, prepare candy clay; let set. Divide clay in 5 portions; tint portions red (match Red Candy Melts), brown, gray, yellow and black. Place mini ball cakes flat side down on cooling grid over pan. Cover with melted red candy (p. 106); let set. Turn cakes over and cover flat side with melted black candy; let set. Make legs and connectors (p. 111). For grate, roll and position 1/8 in. diameter logs of gray clay. For grill rim, roll and position a 1/4 in. diameter log of red clay. Shape two 3/4 in. brown burgers. On waxed paper, roll out yellow clay; cut 1/2 in. square for cheese. Position burgers and cheese. For hot dogs, combine red clay with a little brown; shape and position two 1 1/4 in. hot dogs. For wheels, shape two 1/2 in. black clay disks; attach to legs with melted candy.

*Combine red and green candy colors for brown shown. Use a little black candy color to make gray shown.
†Brand confectionery coating.

Taco Supreme ›

PAN:	Jumbo Muffin,
TIP:	3
COLORS:	Brown, Leaf Green, Orange
RECIPE:	Buttercream Icing, p. 101
ALSO:	Taco Pattern, p. 114; Candy Melts®† in Light Cocoa and Yellow; Chocolate Ready-To-Use Decorator Icing; Parchment Triangles; Pastry Brush; Black Colored Sugar; Cake Release; Spatula; zip-close plastic bag, waxed paper, shredded coconut, maraschino cherries, paring knife

See "Wilton Products", p. 118-127 for most Wilton items used in this project.

Brush pan cavities with Cake Release; bake and cool cupcakes without baking cups. Trim tapered sides straight; cut cupcake horizontally into slices, 3/4 in. deep. Trim one side of each slice straight, 1 1/4 in. from rounded side. Set aside.

Make taco shells. Trace pattern on paper, cover with waxed paper. Combine melted yellow candy with a little melted cocoa candy for yellow shown. Add black sugar for flecks. Using melted candy in cut parchment bag, outline and pipe in pattern; smooth with spatula. Position cupcake piece slightly below top edge of taco; lift paper to fold candy over cupcake piece, forming shell. Refrigerate until firm; peel off paper. Using tip 3, cover cupcake area with chocolate icing. To tint coconut, place in zip-close bags along with a few drops of orange or green color; knead bag. Sprinkle tinted coconut over icing for lettuce and cheese. Cut cherries in small pieces and position.

< A Slice of Summer

PAN: 9 x 13 in. Sheet
COLOR: Kelly Green
FONDANT: White Ready-To-Use Rolled Fondant; Rolling Pin; Roll & Cut Mat
RECIPE: Buttercream Icing, p. 101
ALSO: Candy Melts®† in Red, White and Light Cocoa; Round Comfort Grip™ Cutter; Bold Tip Primary Colors FoodWriter™ Edible Color Markers; Parchment Triangles; Spatula; paring knife, ruler

See "Wilton Products", p. 118-127 for most Wilton items used in this project.

Bake and cool sheet cake using firm-textured batter. Trim to 1 1/2 in. high. Cut out cake using round cutter; cut circles in half. Melt red candy; add a little white to lighten. Using spatula, spread candy over cake; let set. Spread candy on back side; let set. Tint fondant green. Roll out 1/8 in. thick; cut a 1 1/2 x 6 in. rectangle. Position cake on fondant. Spread curved portion of cake with melted white candy and attach fondant; trim as needed. Pipe seeds using melted cocoa candy in cut parchment bag. Draw rind lines with green FoodWriter.

My Piece a Pie >

PANS: Standard Muffin
TIP: 6
COLORS: Brown, No-Taste Red
RECIPE: Buttercream Icing, p. 101
ALSO: White Standard Baking Cups; Spatula; shredded coconut, mini candy-coated chocolate dots, chocolate chips

See "Wilton Products", p. 118-127 for most Wilton items used in this project.

Ice cupcakes smooth. Pipe tip 6 ring around edge; pipe in red buttercream sauce with tip 6. Cut chocolate chips in chunks and green mini chocolates in half for sausage and peppers; position on cupcake. Sprinkle top with coconut for cheese.

‹ Sink or Swim!

PAN: Cookie Sheet
TIPS: 1, 1A, 3, 12
COLORS:* Kelly Green, Rose, Violet, Copper (light skin tone), Brown, Red-Red, Black, Lemon Yellow, Golden Yellow
RECIPE: Buttercream Icing, p. 101
ALSO: Pastel Silicone Baking Cups; Spatula; cornstarch
See "Wilton Products", p. 118-127 for most Wilton items used in this project.

Bake and cool cupcakes in silicone cups supported by cookie sheet. Ice smooth. Decorate using very stiff buttercream. Pipe a tip 1A circle inner tube. Figure pipe kids with tip 1A ball body and head. Pipe in tip 3 bathing suits (pat smooth with finger dipped in cornstarch). Add tip 12 pull-out arms and legs. Pipe tip 3 dot fingers and nose, pull-out or swirl hair. Add tip 1 dot eyes and string mouth.

* Combine Brown with Red-Red for brown shown. Combine Violet with Rose for lavender shown. Combine Lemon Yellow with Golden Yellow for yellow shown.

Smile Markers ›

PAN: Standard Muffin
TIPS: 2, 3
COLORS:* Copper (light skin tone), Brown, Red-Red, Lemon Yellow, Golden Yellow, Black, Christmas Red, Royal Blue, Kelly Green, Violet, Rose
RECIPES: Buttercream, Royal Icings, p. 101
ALSO: Cupcake Heaven Standard Baking Cups; Fine Tip Primary Colors FoodWriter™ Edible Color Markers; Meringue Powder; Spatula
See "Wilton Products", p. 118-127 for most Wilton items used in this project.

Two days in advance: Make 1¹/4 in. diameter puddle faces (p. 111) using thinned royal icing in copper and brown. Let dry.

Ice cupcakes smooth in buttercream. Position faces. Pipe tip 3 outline, pull-out or swirl hair. Print tip 2 name. Draw eyes and mouth using black FoodWriter.

* Combine Brown with Red-Red for brown shown. Combine Lemon Yellow with Golden Yellow for yellow shown. Combine Christmas Red with Red-Red for red shown. Combine Violet with Rose for violet shown.

Kids Take the Wheel!

PAN: Standard Muffin; Cookie Sheet; Cooling Grid

TIPS: 3, 8

COLORS:* Orange, Royal Blue, Violet, Rose, Kelly Green, Copper (skin tone), Lemon Yellow, Golden Yellow, Red-Red, Christmas Red, Black, Brown

RECIPES: Buttercream, Royal Icings, p. 101; Roll-Out Cookie, p. 103

ALSO: White Standard Baking Cups; Colored Sugars in Red, Orange, Blue, Light Green, Lavender, Yellow; 101 Cookie Cutters Set; Fine Tip Primary Colors FoodWriter™ Edible Color Markers; Meringue Powder; Spatula; candy-coated chocolate dots, yellow stick candy, large spice drops, construction paper, ruler, scissors, waxed paper

See "Wilton Products", p. 118-127 for most Wilton items used in this project.

Two days in advance: Make center axle. Roll out cookie dough; using round cutters from set, cut 1 small and 2 large cookies. Bake and cool. Ice cookies smooth; sprinkle small cookie with yellow sugar. Trim 10 candy sticks to 4¹/₂ in. long; sandwich between 2 large cookies using royal icing, spacing evenly to create spokes of wheel. Prop up sticks with crumpled waxed paper pieces and let dry. **Also:** Make 1¹/₈ in. diameter puddle faces (p. 111) using thinned royal icing in copper and brown. Let dry.

Ice cupcakes smooth in white buttercream; ice bottom half of 2 each in blue, red, green, orange and violet. Sprinkle color areas with matching colored sugar. Pipe a tip 8 line across center; position candy-coated chocolates and faces. Pipe tip 3 swirl, outline or pull-out hair. Draw eyes and mouth with black FoodWriter. Position small cookie on sandwich cookies. Position candy-coated chocolates. For base of wheel, cut paper in a cone shape, 12 in. high, 9 in. wide at bottom and 2 in. wide at top. Position axle; position cupcakes at end of spokes. Position spice drops at base.

*Combine Violet with Rose for violet shown. Combine Lemon Yellow with Golden Yellow for yellow shown. Combine Red-Red with Christmas Red for red shown. Combine Brown with Red-Red for brown shown.

The Farm Team

PANS: Standard Muffin; Mini Muffin; Cookie Sheet; Cooling Grid

TIPS: 2, 2A, 5, 13, 349, 352

COLORS:* Black, Brown, Red-Red, Rose, Royal Blue, Orange, Lemon Yellow, Golden Yellow

RECIPES: Buttercream Icing, p. 101; Roll-Out Cookie, p. 103

ALSO: White Standard, Mini Baking Cups; Round, Square Cut-Outs™; Rolling Pin; Spatula; cornstarch

See "Wilton Products", p. 118-127 for most Wilton items used in this project.

In advance: Roll out cookie dough. For horse, pig, sheep and cow, cut heads using medium round Cut-Out; shape horse head slightly longer and narrower. Cut all legs using medium square Cut-Out. Cut square in half, then each piece in thirds; separate. For chicken and chicks, cut heads using wide end of tip 2A. Bake and cool all cookies.

Bake and cool chicken and chick cupcakes in mini pan, others in standard pan. On all except sheep, ice heads and legs smooth in same color as cupcake; position head and legs. For horse, pipe tip 5 outline hooves and head marking. Pipe tip 2 dot eyes, nose and pull-out hair. Add tip 352 pull-out ears. For pig and cow, pipe tip 5 ball muzzle (pat smooth with finger dipped in cornstarch). Add tip 2 dot nose, string mouth and hooves. Pipe tip 352 pull-out ears. For cow, add tip 349 inside ears; pipe in tip 5 bell with tip 2 outline string. Add tip 2 spots and dot eyes. For sheep, cover cupcake with tip 13 C-motion swirl wool. Ice head and legs smooth; position. Pipe tip 5 bead ears, outline hooves. Add tip 2 dot eyes and nose, outline mouth and inside ears. Pipe tip 13 swirl wool on head. For chickens and chicks, pipe tip 352 pull-out wings. Pipe tip 2 dot eyes and pull-out hair, feet and beak.

*Combine Lemon Yellow with Golden Yellow for yellow shown. Combine Brown with Red-Red for brown shown.

‹ Creature Cruise

PANS: Cookie Sheet; Cooling Grid
TIPS: 1, 3
COLORS:* Lemon Yellow, Golden Yellow, Leaf Green, Orange, Black
RECIPES: Buttercream Icing, p. 101; Roll-Out Cookie, p. 103
ALSO: Diamond Silicone Baking Cups; Square Cut-Outs™; Noah's Ark Mini Cookie Cutters; White Candy Melts®†; Rolling Pin; Spatula; paring knife

See "Wilton Products", p. 118-127 for most Wilton items used in this project.

In advance: Tint portions of dough yellow, orange, black, gray and green. Thin black and portions of orange and green to piping consistency. Roll out dough; cut animals. Cut cabin using medium square Cut-Out. For roof, cut a square using largest Cut-Out; cut horizontally in thirds. Cut sides of each third at an angle to taper. Using thinned dough, pipe tip 1 dot eyes and spots, tip 3 pipe-in hair, outline ear and cabin windows. Bake and cool.

Bake and cool cupcakes in silicone cups supported by cookie sheet; ice smooth. Attach roof to cabin cookie with melted candy. Attach cookies with icing.

*Combine Lemon Yellow with Golden Yellow for yellow shown. Combine Leaf Green with Lemon Yellow for green shown.

Pet Projects ›

PAN: Standard Muffin
TIP: 12
COLOR: Golden Yellow
RECIPE: Buttercream Icing, p. 101
ALSO: Cupcake Heaven Standard Baking Cups; Decorator Brush Set; Candy Melts®† in Yellow, Light Cocoa; candy-coated chocolate dots, chocolate nougat candies, uncooked spaghetti, scissors, waxed paper

See "Wilton Products", p. 118-127 for most Wilton items used in this project.

Ice cupcakes smooth. Pipe tip 12 dot muzzle. Shape a small piece of nougat candy for nose and position. Position candy-coated chocolate dot eyes. For dog ears, shape nougat candy; position. For cat ears, cut yellow Candy Melts wafer to shape; position. For cat whiskers, paint pieces of spaghetti with melted cocoa candy; let dry on waxed paper. Insert in muzzle.

† Brand confectionery coating.

‹ Moby Quick!

PANS: Jumbo Muffin; Cookie Sheet; Cooling Grid
TIPS: 5, 16
COLORS: Sky Blue, Royal Blue, Black
RECIPES: Buttercream, Royal Icings, p. 101; Roll-Out Cookie, p. 103
ALSO: Water Spout Pattern, p. 114; White Jumbo Baking Cups; Nesting Heart Cutter Set; Rolling Pin; Meringue Powder; Spatula; waxed paper, cornstarch

See "Wilton Products", p. 118-127 for most Wilton items used in this project.

One day in advance: Make water spout. Cover pattern with waxed paper; pipe tip 5 spout using royal icing (make extras to allow for breakage). Let dry overnight. Roll out dough; cut cookie tail using second smallest heart cutter. Bake and cool.

Attach cookie to cupcake with buttercream. Ice cupcake smooth to level of cookie. Insert water spout. Outline and pipe in tip 5 mouth (smooth with finger dipped in cornstarch). Cover cupcake and cookie with tip 16 stars. Overpipe tip 5 dot eyes and spots (flatten and smooth with finger dipped in cornstarch).

Up in Arms ›

PANS: Cookie Sheet; Cooling Grid
TIPS: 2, 3, 9
COLORS:* Violet, Black, Royal Blue, Rose
RECIPES: Buttercream, Royal Icings, p. 101; Roll-Out Cookie, p. 103
ALSO: Legs Pattern, p. 114; Pastel Silicone Baking Cups; Round Cut-Outs™; 4 in. Lollipop Sticks; Rolling Pin; Meringue Powder; Spatula; toothpick, paring knife, waxed paper

See "Wilton Products", p. 118-127 for most Wilton items used in this project.

One day in advance: Tint cookie dough violet; roll out and cut head cookie using largest round Cut-Out. For 8 legs, trace pattern on dough with toothpick; reverse for 4 legs. Cut using paring knife. Bake and cool all cookies.

Position head cookie on waxed paper. Using royal icing, outline and pipe in tip 9 hat; add tip 9 outline brim, tip 2 section lines and dot button. Pipe tip 2 outline mouth; add tip 3 dot eyes and cheeks (flatten and smooth with finger dipped in cornstarch). Pipe tip 2 dot pupils.

Bake and cool cupcakes in silicone cups supported by cookie sheet. Ice cupcakes smooth in buttercream. Cut cookie stick to 3 in.; attach to head cookie with dots of royal icing and insert in cupcake. Insert leg cookies.

*Combine Violet with Rose for violet shown.

‹ One Fast Turtle!

PAN: Standard Muffin
TIP: 2
COLORS:* Lemon Yellow, Leaf Green, Black
RECIPE: Buttercream Icing, p. 101
ALSO: White Standard Baking Cups; chocolate nougat candies, candy-coated chocolate dots, round fruit jellies

See "Wilton Products", p. 118-127 for most Wilton items used in this project.

Ice cupcakes smooth. Position fruit jelly head; ice smooth. Position candy-coated chocolate spots. Cut nougat candy sections horizontally in half, then vertically in half; position for legs. Pipe tip 2 dot eyes and outline smile.

* Combine Leaf Green with Lemon Yellow for green shown.

School's in Session! ›

PAN: Cookie Sheet
TIP: 5
COLORS:* Orange, Rose, Lemon Yellow, Golden Yellow, Royal Blue
CANDY: White Candy Melts®†, Primary Candy Color Set**
RECIPE: Buttercream Icing, p. 101
ALSO: Top Fin, Side and Tail Fin Patterns, p. 114; Pastel Silicone Baking Cups; Parchment Triangles; waxed paper, cornstarch

See "Wilton Products", p. 118-127 for most Wilton items used in this project.

In advance: Make candy trims. Cover fin patterns with waxed paper. Tint portions of melted white candy yellow, green, violet and black using candy colors. With melted candy in cut parchment bag, outline and pipe in top, side and tail fins for each cupcake. On waxed paper, pipe a white dot eye with a black dot pupil using melted candy in cut parchment bag. Refrigerate candy until firm.

Bake and cool cupcakes in silicone cups supported by cookie sheet. Ice smooth in blue. With tip 5, pipe in fish area in orange, rose or yellow (pat smooth with finger dipped in cornstarch). Insert fins in cupcake; position eyes.

* Combine Lemon Yellow with Golden Yellow for yellow shown.
** Combine Green with Yellow candy color for green shown.
† Brand confectionery coating.

First Birthday Bear >

PANS: Standard Muffin; Mini Muffin
TIPS: 2, 4, 12, 101
COLORS: Rose, Black
RECIPE: Buttercream Icing, p. 101
ALSO: Ready-To-Use Chocolate Decorator Icing; White Standard Baking Cups; White Mini Baking Cups; Shower Rattles; Spatula; vanilla wafer cookies, cornstarch

See "Wilton Products", p. 118-127 for most Wilton items used in this project.

Bake and cool 2 standard cupcakes and 4 mini cupcakes for each bear. Using chocolate icing, ice smooth 1 standard cupcake thick for head; insert 2 wafer cookies for ears. Using tip 12, cover remaining cupcakes with icing; smooth with spatula. Overpipe muzzle area. Outline and pipe in nose, ears, inside ears and bib with tip 4 (smooth with finger dipped in cornstarch). Pipe tip 4 outline mouth, dot eyes and pads of feet (flatten and smooth with finger dipped in cornstarch). Pipe tip 101 ruffle; add tip 2 message. Position rattle.

‹ The Treat Train

PANS: Cookie Sheet; Cooling Grid
TIPS: 1M (2110), 3, 8, 12, 32
COLORS: Royal Blue, Golden Yellow, Violet, Rose, Orange
RECIPES: Buttercream Icing, p. 101; Roll-Out Cookie, p. 103
ALSO: Square Silicone Baking Cups; Round, Square Cut-Outs™; Jumbo Confetti, Sour Cherry Balls Sprinkle Decorations; Rolling Pin; Spatula; large spice drops, candy-coated chocolate dots, candy-coated fruit-shaped candies, spice drops, cornstarch

See "Wilton Products", p. 118-127 for most Wilton items used in this project.

Prepare cookie dough; tint ½ blue. Divide remaining dough in 4ths; tint orange, rose, yellow and violet. Roll out dough. Cut 4 blue squares using largest Cut-Out; for violet roof, cut a square ¼ in. larger on all sides than Cut-Out. Cut 4 large engine wheels in yellow using medium round Cut-Out. Using wide end of tip 1M, cut 4 small wheels for each car and 2 for engine front in yellow, rose and orange.

Bake and cool cupcakes in silicone cups supported by cookie sheet. Cover top of engine front with tip 12 zigzags; overpipe. Smooth with spatula to form semi-circle shape. Attach large spice drop smokestack with icing; for headlight, cut large yellow spice drop in half and attach with icing. For engine cab, ice cupcake top smooth; trim blue cookies to fit upright on cupcake and attach sides with icing. Let set. Pipe tip 3 zigzag window (smooth with finger dipped in cornstarch). Outline with tip 3; pipe tip 3 beads along cab seams. Attach roof to cab with icing. Cover cars with tip 32 swirls. Position candies. Attach wheel cookies with icing; attach jumbo confetti axle to each.

Jolly Juggler ›

PANS: Standard Muffin; Mini Muffin
TIPS: 16, 32
COLORS:* Copper (skin tone), Lemon Yellow, Golden Yellow
CANDY: Candy Melts®† in White and Red; Primary, Garden Candy Color Sets; Alphabet/Numbers Mold; 4 in. Lollipop Sticks
RECIPE: Buttercream Icing, p. 101
ALSO: Hat, Hair, Foot, Bow Tie, Button, Cheek, Eye, Hand, Mouth Patterns, p. 114; White Standard, Mini Baking Cups; Colored Sugars in Blue, Red, Light Green, Violet, Orange, Dark Green; Parchment Triangles; red gumball, waxed paper

See "Wilton Products", p. 118-127 for most Wilton items used in this project.

In advance: Make candy trims. Tint portions of melted white candy blue, orange, pink, yellow, green and black using candy colors. Trace patterns on parchment paper (reverse to make 2nd hand, foot and hair sections). Cover with waxed paper. Pipe in hands, feet, bow tie and buttons with melted candy in cut parchment bag; sprinkle with matching colored sugar and refrigerate until firm. Pipe in hat, eyes, pupils, mouth, cheeks and hair; refrigerate until firm. Pipe dots on hat; sprinkle with sugar and refrigerate until firm. Attach hat, hands and feet to lollipop stick with melted candy; let set. Mold name letters; refrigerate until firm.

Use standard cupcakes for head and tummy, mini cupcakes for arms, legs and name balls. Cover arms, legs and tummy with tip 32 swirl. Position bow tie, buttons and knot. Insert hands and feet. Pipe tip 16 zigzag cuffs. Ice head smooth; insert hat. Pipe tip 16 zigzag brim and rosette pompom. Position eyes, gumball nose, mouth, cheeks and hair. Ice name balls smooth; dip in matching colored sugar. Position letters.

* Combine Lemon Yellow with Golden Yellow for yellow shown.

‹ Solo Flight

TIPS: 1, 2, 32
COLORS: Black, Brown, Copper (skin tone), Lemon Yellow
CANDY: White Candy Melts®†; Primary, Garden Candy Color Sets
RECIPES: Buttercream Icing, p. 101; favorite crisped rice cereal treats
ALSO: Wing, Tail Fins, Propeller, Bolt Patterns, p. 115; Colored Sugars in Green, Blue, Orange; Parchment Triangles; Rolling Pin; Cake Board; sugar ice cream cones, granulated sugar, round wafer candies, large red spice drops, waxed paper, paring knife

See "Wilton Products", p. 118-127 for most Wilton items used in this project.

Prepare cereal treats and fill sugar cones; set aside. Trace patterns on paper (you will need 2 wings and 3 tail fins for each treat); tape to cake board and cover with waxed paper. Tint portions of candy green, blue and orange using candy colors. Using melted candy in cut parchment bag, fill in patterns; refrigerate until firm. Turn over all pieces and overpipe with melted candy for dimension; sprinkle with matching colored sugar and refrigerate until firm. Reserve melted candy for attaching candy pieces. In buttercream, pipe tip 32 swirl on cones.

Assemble plane on waxed paper-covered board. Pipe a little melted candy on board and position cone on top to stabilize. Attach 2 tail fins horizontally to cone; refrigerate until firm. Attach vertical tail fin; support with spice drops on either side. Fill in gaps between spice drops and vertical fin with melted candy; sprinkle with sugar and refrigerate until firm. Attach wings, supporting with spice drops cut to fit; refrigerate until firm. Make and attach pilot (p. 111). Attach bolt to propeller with melted candy; attach propeller to cone with icing.

† Brand confectionery coating

Follow That Car! ›

PAN: Standard Muffin
TIPS: 1, 2, 3, 4, 6, 9
COLORS:* Red-Red, Chrismas Red, Kelly Green, Royal Blue, Black, Brown, Copper (skin tone)
RECIPES: Buttercream, Royal Icings, p. 101
ALSO: White Standard Baking Cups; Meringue Powder; Parchment Triangles; hollow-center fruit-flavored candies, spice drops, mini candy-coated chocolates, cornstarch, waxed paper

See "Wilton Products", p. 118-127 for most Wilton items used in this project.

Two days in advance: Using thinned royal icing, pipe 3/4 in. diameter puddle face (p. 111) on waxed paper. Let dry.

Ice cupcakes smooth in white buttercream. Overpipe side of car with tip 6 (smooth with finger dipped in cornstarch). Pipe tip 9 outline roof; add tip 6 outline window bar. Pipe in tip 2 shirt. Position puddle face. Pipe tip 2 dot eyes, string mouth and pull-out hair. Pipe tip 2 outline steering column and wheel. Pipe in tip 4 grass under car (smooth with finger dipped in cornstarch). Position hollow-center candy wheels and candy-coated chocolate hubcaps. Pipe tip 3 outline door handle. Trim spice drop to 1/8 in. high; attach with dots of icing for headlight.

*Combine Red-Red with Christmas Red for red shown. Combine Brown with Red-Red for brown shown.

< Clown in the Clouds

PAN: Cookie Sheet
TIPS: 3, 21
COLORS: Royal Blue, Red-Red, Kelly Green
FONDANT: White Ready-To-Use Rolled Fondant; Rolling Pin; Roll & Cut Mat
RECIPE: Buttercream Icing, p. 101
ALSO: Pastel Silicone Baking Cups; 8 in. Lollipop Sticks; Small Derby Clown Heads; Cake Board; Spatula; 9 in. balloons, cornstarch

See "Wilton Products", p. 118-127 for most Wilton items used in this project.

In advance: Make 3 balloon rests for each cupcake. Tint portions of fondant blue, red and green; roll out 1/8 in. thick. Cut circles using smallest Cut-Out; let dry on cornstarch-dusted board.

Bake and cool cupcakes in silicone cups supported by cookie sheet. Ice smooth. Attach a balloon rest to end of 3 sticks with icing. Insert sticks diagonally into cupcake to form a triangle opening for balloon. Pipe tip 21 ball body; add tip 21 pull-out arms. Pipe tip 3 ball hands. Insert clown head. Position balloon on sticks.

Hello, Copter! >

PANS: Jumbo Muffin; Cookie Sheet; Cooling Grid
TIPS: 3, 6, 16
COLORS:* Red-Red, Christmas Red, Lemon Yellow, Golden Yellow, Violet, Brown, Copper (skin tone)
RECIPES: Buttercream, Royal Icings, p. 101; Roll-Out Cookie, p. 103
ALSO: A-B-C and 1-2-3 Cutter Set; Jumbo Baking Cups; Fine Tip Primary Colors FoodWriter™ Edible Color Markers; Meringue Powder; Rolling Pin; Parchment Triangles; Spatula; granulated sugar, waxed paper, scissors, purple spice drops

See "Wilton Products", p. 118-127 for most Wilton items used in this project.

Two days in advance: Using thinned royal icing in cut parchment bag, pipe 3/4 in. diameter puddle face (p. 111), on waxed paper. Let dry.

Tint a portion of cookie dough violet. Roll out plain and violet dough. Cut main propeller using "X" cutter and violet dough; cut tail using "J" cutter from set and plain dough. Roll a small ball of violet dough and position for bolt on propeller. Bake and cool.

Attach tail cookie to cupcake with icing. Ice cupcake smooth in buttercream to level of cookie. Pipe tip 6 outline window frame. Cover tail and area outside window frame with tip 16 stars. Draw eyes and mouth on face using black FoodWriter; position on cupcake. Add tip 3 swirl hair. Roll out spice drops on waxed paper sprinkled with sugar. With scissors, cut strips for back propeller and a small ball for top bolt. Attach tail propeller pieces and main propeller cookie with dots of icing.

* Combine Red-Red with Christmas Red for red shown. Combine Lemon Yellow with Golden Yellow for yellow shown. Combine Brown with Red-Red for brown shown.

Luscious Loot

PAN: Cookie Sheet

TIPS: 2, 5

COLORS: Black, Red-Red, Copper (skin tone)

RECIPES: Royal Icing, p. 101; favorite brownie mix

ALSO: Diamond Silicone Baking Cups; 6 in. Lollipop Sticks; Parchment Triangles; Meringue Powder; candy-coated chocolate dots, spice drops, white cardstock, waxed paper, scissors, ruler, double-stick tape

See "Wilton Products", p. 118-127 for most Wilton items used in this project.

Two days in advance: Using thinned royal icing, pipe 1 1/4 in. diameter puddle face (p. 111) on waxed paper. Let dry. **Also in advance:** On faces, make hat. Using royal icing, outline and pipe in hat shape with tip 5; let dry. Pipe tip 2 dot eye and patch, string mouth and strap using royal icing; let dry.

Bake and cool brownies 3/4 in. high in silicone cups supported by cookie sheet. For sail, cut cardstock triangle, 2 3/4 in. at bottom and 3 1/2 in. on angled sides; cut 1/4 in. off bottom from left side to center. Trim lollipop stick to 5 1/2 in.; attach sail with tape. Attach face with royal icing; let dry. Insert in brownie. Fill cup to top with candy.

‹ Swashbuckler

PAN:	Standard Muffin
TIPS:	3, 6
COLORS:	Red-Red, Copper (skin tone), Black
FONDANT:	Primary Colors Fondant Multi Pack; Heart Cut-Outs™; Rolling Pin; Roll & Cut Mat
RECIPES:	Buttercream Icing, p. 101
ALSO:	White Standard Baking Cups; Cake Boards; Spatula; cornstarch

See "Wilton Products", p. 118-127 for most Wilton items used in this project.

In advance: Make headwrap tails. Roll out red fondant 1/8 in. thick. Cut 2 hearts using smallest Cut-Out. Let dry on cornstarch-dusted board.

Ice cupcakes smooth. Pipe in tip 6 headwrap (pat smooth with finger dipped in cornstarch). Attach headwrap tails with dots of icing. Outline and pipe in eye patch with tip 3; pipe tip 3 outline strap. Pipe tip 3 outline mouth and dot cheeks, nose, eyes and pupils. Add tip 3 dots on headwrap.

Treasure Trove ›

PANS:	Petite Loaf; Cookie Sheet; Cooling Grid
TIP:	4
COLORS:	Golden Yellow
RECIPES:	Buttercream Icing, p. 101; Chocolate Roll-Out Cookie, p. 103
ALSO:	Rolling Pin; Chocolate Ready-To-Use Decorator Icing; Cake Release; Pastry Brush; rock candy, candy-coated chocolate dots, foil-wrapped chocolate coins, toothpick, paring knife

See "Wilton Products", p. 118-127 for most Wilton items used in this project.

Roll out cookie dough. Using knife, cut a 3¼ x 2¼ in. rectangle lid. Bake and cool. Brush loaf pan with Cake Release; bake and cool loaf cakes without cups. Ice cakes smooth with chocolate icing. Pipe tip 4 outline rims on cake and cookie; add tip 4 dot lock. Position candy on cake top. Position cookie, supporting with candy and trimming as needed to fit cake. Pipe tip 4 outline on back rim as needed to support cookie.

< Looking a Bit Spacey

PANS:	Mini Muffin; Cookie Sheet; Cooling Grid
TIPS:	1, 2, 5, 349
COLORS:*	Leaf Green, Lemon Yellow, Black
FONDANT:	Primary Colors Fondant Multi Pack; Round Cut-Outs™; Rolling Pin; Roll & Cut Mat
RECIPES:	Buttercream Icing, p. 101; Roll-Out Cookie, p. 103
ALSO:	Pastel Silicone Baking Cups; Comfort Grip™ Round Cutter; 4 in. Lollipop Sticks; Rolling Pin; Parchment Triangles; Cake Release; Pastry Brush; Cake Board; Spatula; small gumballs, craft knife, scissors, cornstarch

See "Wilton Products", p. 118-127 for most Wilton items used in this project.

In advance: Make spaceship lights. Roll out fondant 1/8 in. thick; cut circles with smallest Cut-Out. Let dry on cornstarch-dusted board. Tint cookie dough dark gray. Roll out and cut cookies with round cutter; bake and cool.

Bake and cool standard cupcakes in silicone cups supported by cookie sheet. Brush mini pan with Cake Release; bake and cool mini cupcakes with no baking cups. Ice smooth. Position cookie on standard cupcake. Position mini, bottom side up, on cookie. Pipe tip 5 band at base of mini. Pipe tip 5 ball face (flatten and smooth with finger dipped in cornstarch). Pipe tip 349 pull-out ears. Add tip 2 dot eyes and nose, tip 1 outline eyebrows, mouth and dot pupils. Attach lights to side of cookie with tip 2 dots of icing. Using knife, cut hole in gumball; trim lollipop stick to 2½ in. and insert. Insert stick in cupcake.

*Combine Leaf Green with Lemon Yellow for green shown.

Dine with Dino >

PANS:	Jumbo Muffin; Cookie Sheet; Cooling Grid
TIPS:	2, 16
COLORS:*	Leaf Green, Lemon Yellow, Black
RECIPES:	Buttercream Icing, p. 101; Roll-Out Cookie, p. 103
ALSO:	Dinosaur Head, Leg and Tail Patterns, p. 115; White Jumbo Baking Cups; Rolling Pin; Parchment Triangles; waxed paper, paring knife, scissors, granulated sugar, spice drops, toothpick

See "Wilton Products", p. 118-127 for most Wilton items used in this project.

In advance: Roll out cookie dough. With toothpick, trace head and tail patterns; cut cookies with knife. Bake and cool.

Ice cupcake smooth; position cookies. Add icing to level of cookies. Cover cupcakes and cookies with tip 16 stars. Trace leg areas with toothpick. Pipe and overpipe legs with tip 16 stars. For spikes, roll out purple spice drops on waxed paper sprinkled with granulated sugar; cut triangles in various sizes and insert. For spots, cut orange spice drops horizontally in 3rds. Flatten, shape and dip in sugar; position. For toes, cut small pieces from purple spice drops; position. Pipe tip 2 dot eyes and pupils, outline smile.

*Combine Leaf Green with Lemon Yellow for green shown.

Screamin' Demons!

PAN: Cookie Sheet

TIPS: 1, 2A, 3, 4

COLORS: * Orange, Black, Lemon Yellow, Golden Yellow, Red-Red, Christmas Red, Leaf Green, Violet, Rose

RECIPE: Buttercream Icing, p. 101

ALSO: Demon Hand Pattern, p. 114; Pastel Silicone Baking Cups; Rolling Pin; Spatula; spice drops, candy-coated fruit-shaped candies, taffy (not salt water), candy-coated chocolate dots, white hollow-center hard candies, yellow stick candy, granulated sugar, cornstarch, waxed paper, scissors, paring knife

See "Wilton Products", p. 118-127 for most Wilton items used in this project.

Bake and cool cupcakes in silicone cups supported by cookie sheet; ice smooth. For orange demon, pipe tip 2A ball eyes with tip 3 dot pupils (pat smooth with finger dipped in cornstarch). Position candy-coated chocolate nose. Pipe tip 4 outline mouth; outline and pipe in tip 3 teeth (pat smooth with finger dipped in cornstarch). For hair, roll out 2 spice drops on waxed paper sprinkled with sugar. Cut two 1 x 1 1/2 in. strips; cut fringe 3/4 in. deep with scissors. Roll strips up to form hair tufts; insert in cupcake top, adjusting fringe for fuller hair. For yellow demon, position hollow-center candy eye; attach candy-coated chocolate pupil with icing. Pipe tip 1 outline veins. Pipe tip 4 outline mouth; pipe in tip 3 tooth (pat smooth with finger dipped in cornstarch). For arms, cut yellow candy sticks in 2 in. lengths; insert in cupcake. For each hand, roll out 2 spice drops; using pattern and knife, cut hands. Attach hands to arms by pressing in place. Make hair following directions for orange demon. For green demon, make eyes, pupils and mouth and position candy nose as for orange demon. Insert banana-shaped candies for horns. Pipe tip 3 dot spots (flatten and smooth with finger dipped in cornstarch). Shape taffy to form tongue; position.

*Combine Lemon Yellow with Golden Yellow for yellow shown. Combine Red-Red with Christmas Red for red shown. Combine Violet with Rose for violet shown. Combine Leaf Green with Lemon Yellow for green shown.

< Tee Time

PAN:	Standard Muffin
TIP:	233
COLORS:	Kelly Green, Red-Red
FONDANT:	White Ready-To-Use Rolled Fondant; Round Cut-Outs™; Rolling Pin; Roll & Cut Mat
RECIPES:	Buttercream Icing, p. 101; Thinned Fondant Adhesive, p. 102
ALSO:	White Standard Baking Cups; 4 in. Lollipop Sticks; Cake Board; Gum-Tex™; waxed paper, cornstarch

See "Wilton Products", p. 118-127 for most Wilton items used in this project.

Add $1/2$ teaspoon Gum-Tex to 4 oz. fondant. Trim lollipop stick to 3 in. Tint a portion of white fondant red; shape into $1^1/2$ in. long tee around top half of lollipop stick. Let dry on cornstarch-dusted board. Roll out white fondant $1/4$ in. thick; cut golf ball using medium Cut-Out. Imprint dimples with lollipop stick. Let dry. Attach ball to tee using fondant adhesive; let dry. Cover tops of cupcakes with tip 233 pull-out grass. Insert tee.

Grab the Facemask! >

PAN:	Standard Muffin
TIPS:	6, 9, 16
COLORS:	Royal Blue, Red-Red
RECIPES:	Buttercream, Royal Icings, p. 101
ALSO:	Facemask Pattern, p. 114; Football Standard Baking Cups; Meringue Powder; Spatula; waxed paper

See "Wilton Products", p. 118-127 for most Wilton items used in this project.

In advance: Make facemask. Cover pattern with waxed paper. Using royal icing and tip 6, outline pattern; let dry at least 24 hours.

Ice cupcakes smooth in buttercream. Outline helmet with tip 9. Fill in with tip 16 stars. Position facemask. Overpipe back point of facemask with tip 16 stars. Add tip 9 dot ear hole.

< Just Kickin' Back

PAN:	Standard Muffin
TIPS:	3, 13
COLOR:	Black
RECIPE:	Buttercream Icing, p. 101
ALSO:	Soccer Ball Pattern, p. 114; Soccer Standard Baking Cups; Cooling Grid; Spatula; toothpick

See "Wilton Products", p. 118-127 for most Wilton items used in this project.

Ice cupcakes smooth. Trace soccer ball pattern with toothpick. Outline pattern with tip 3; fill in alternating sections with tip 13 stars.

‹ Winning Every Inning!

PANS:	Standard Muffin; Mini Muffin
TIPS:	2, 6, 8
COLOR:	Royal Blue, Christmas Red
FONDANT:	Primary Colors Fondant Multi Pack; Rolling Pin; Roll & Cut Mat
RECIPE:	Buttercream Icing, p. 101
ALSO:	White Standard, Mini Baking Cups; Circle Metal Cutter; Cake Board; Spatula; cornstarch, waxed paper, toothpicks

See "Wilton Products", p. 118-127 for most Wilton items used in this project.

In advance: Make cap brims. Roll out red fondant 1/8 in. thick. Cut circle using cutter; cut a crescent shaped brim from circle, 1/4 in. wide in center. Let dry on waxed paper-covered board sprinkled with cornstarch.

Ice mini cupcakes smooth. Pipe tip 2 outline stitches. Cut a slit in the crown of standard cupcakes, 1 in. deep, at edge of baking cup; insert brim, extending 3/4 in. from edge. Build up icing for cap; smooth. Mark edge of cap in 8 equal sections. Pipe tip 2 section lines from division marks to top of cap. Pipe tip 6 ball button (flatten and smooth with finger dippped in cornstarch).

Post-Game Celebration ›

PAN:	Standard Muffin
TIPS:	10, 233
COLOR:	Kelly Green
RECIPES:	Buttercream, Royal Icings, p. 101
ALSO:	Goal Post Pattern, p. 115; Football Standard Baking Cups; Football Icing Decorations; Meringue Powder; Cake Board; waxed paper, cellophane tape

See "Wilton Products", p. 118-127 for most Wilton items used in this project.

At least 2 days in advance: Make goal posts. Tape pattern to cake board and cover with waxed paper. Using royal icing and tip 10, outline pattern; let dry.

Cover cupcake tops with tip 233 grass in buttercream. Insert goal post and position icing decoration.

‹ Ready for Dunking

PANS:	King-Size Muffin; Cookie Sheet; Cooling Grid
TIP:	5
COLORS:*	Terra Cotta, Golden Yellow, Brown
RECIPES:	Royal Icing, p. 101; Roll-Out Cookie, p. 103; Candy Clay, p. 102
ALSO:	Candy Melts®† in White and Red; Fine Tip Primary Colors FoodWriter™ Edible Color Markers; Round Comfort Grip™ Cutter; 4 in. Lollipop Sticks; Meringue Powder; Pastry Brush; Cake Release; paring knife

See "Wilton Products", p. 118-127 for most Wilton items used in this project.

Prepare red candy clay. For basketball cookies, tint cookie dough brown; roll out. Cut with round cutter; bake and cool. Draw lines with black FoodWriter. Attach lollipop stick with melted candy, leaving 2 in. at bottom. Bake and cool cupcakes without baking cups in pan brushed with Cake Release. Trim to 2 1/2 in. high. Cover with melted white candy (p. 106); let set and repeat. Using royal icing, pipe tip 5 lattice net. Roll candy clay into 1/4 in. diameter rope. Attach for rim with melted candy. Make small hole in center of cupcake; insert basketball.

*Combine Terra Cotta, Golden Yellow and Brown for brown shown.
†Brand confectionary coating.

⌃Laughing Ladybugs

PAN: Mini Muffin
TIPS: 2, 5, 8, 9
COLORS:* Black, Leaf Green, Lemon Yellow, Orange, Red-Red
FONDANT: White Ready-To-Use Rolled Fondant; Rolling Pin; Roll & Cut Mat; Brush Set
RECIPE: Buttercream Icing, p. 101
ALSO: White Mini Baking Cups; Roll & Cut Mat; Spatula; paring knife

See "Wilton Products," p. 118-127 for most Wilton items used in this project.

Ice cupcakes smooth. Tint portion of fondant black; roll out black and white fondant 1/8 in. thick. Cut a thin strip for wing division; position at center of cupcake. For face, roll a 1/2 in. ball of fondant; position on cupcake, pressing lightly to widen. For spots, cut dots using narrow end of tip 8; position. Cut eyes with narrow end of tip 9,

pupils with narrow end of tip 5; attach with damp brush. Pipe tip 2 outline mouth.

* Combine Leaf Green with Lemon Yellow for green shown.

‹Don't Bee Stingy!

PANS: Standard Muffin
TIPS: 5, 9, 233
COLORS: Lemon Yellow, Black
FONDANT: White Ready-To-Use Rolled Fondant; Rolling Pin; Roll & Cut Mat; Brush Set
RECIPE: Buttercream Icing, p. 101
ALSO: White Standard Baking Cups; Nesting Heart Plastic Cutter Set; Fine Tip, Neon Colors FoodWriter™ Edible Color Markers; Clear Vanilla Extract; Cake Boards; 4 in. Lollipop Sticks; waxed paper, cornstarch, uncooked spaghetti, paring knife

See "Wilton Products", p. 118-127 for most Wilton items used in this project.

In advance: Make antennae. Using black icing color, tint a little vanilla and brush on spaghetti; let dry. **Also:** Make fondant stinger and wings. Tint a portion of fondant black. Roll out black and white fondant ⅛ in. thick. Cut a ¾ in. high triangle for stinger. Cut 2 wings using 2nd smallest heart cutter. Let all dry on waxed paper-covered board dusted with cornstarch.

Cover cupcakes with tip 233 pull-out hair in alternating colors. For head, tint fondant yellow, roll a 1½ in. diameter ball. Insert a 2½ in. lollipop stick in bottom of head, leaving 1½ in. extended. Roll out white, black and yellow fondant ⅛ in. thick. Cut eyes and cheeks using narrow end of tip 9, pupils and nose using narrow end of tip 5. Attach to head with damp brush. Draw mouth with black FoodWriter. Cut antennae to 1 in. long; roll ¼ in. black fondant balls for antenna ends. Insert antennae in balls and insert in head. Position head, stinger and wings.

‹Beautiful Butterfly

PANS: Standard Muffin
TIPS: 4, 5, 9
COLORS: Lemon Yellow, Rose, Violet, Black
FONDANT: White Ready-To-Use Rolled Fondant; Rolling Pin; Roll & Cut Mat; Brush Set
RECIPE: Buttercream Icing, p. 101
ALSO: White Standard Baking Cups; Nesting Heart Plastic Cutter Set; Fine Tip Neon Colors Food Writer™ Edible Color Markers; Clear Vanilla Extract; Cake Boards; waxed paper, cornstarch, uncooked spaghetti

See "Wilton Products", p. 118-127 for most Wilton items used in this project.

In advance: Make antennae. Thin black color with a little vanilla and brush on spaghetti. **Also:** Make wings. Tint portions of fondant yellow, violet, rose and black; reserve some white. Roll out yellow fondant ⅛ in. thick; using 3rd smallest cutter, cut 2 heart wings for each butterfly. Cut ½ in. off tip of each heart; let dry on waxed paper-covered cake board dusted with cornstarch. Draw designs using FoodWriters.

Ice cupcakes smooth. Roll 1 in. and ⅝ in. balls of rose fondant, ¾ and ½ in. balls of violet fondant for body sections and head. Roll out white, black and rose fondant ⅛ in. thick; cut eyes and cheeks using narrow end of tip 9, pupils using narrow end of tip 4, nose using narrow end of tip 5. Attach to head using damp brush. Draw mouth with FoodWriter. Trim antennae to ¾ in.; attach ¼ in. balls of black fondant and insert in head. Position head and body sections on cupcake; insert fondant wings on an angle. Support with small piece of fondant if needed.

Inchworm By the Yard!^

PAN: Cookie Sheet
TIP: 3, 21
COLORS:* Violet, Rose, Royal Blue, Lemon Yellow, Orange, Black
RECIPE: Buttercream Icing, p. 101
ALSO: Silly-Feet Baking Cups (2 pks.); 6 in. Lollipop Sticks; Decorator Brush Set; Clear Vanilla Extract; mini candy-coated chocolate dots, small gum balls, paring knife

See "Wilton Products", p. 118-127 for most Wilton items used in this project.

In advance: Bake and cool cupcakes in Silly-Feet cups supported by cookie sheet. Add a little vanilla extract to black icing color. Paint 2 lollipop sticks for antennae; let dry. Heavily ice cupcakes smooth, building up in center. Cover with tip 21 pull-out stars. Cut a hole in 2 gumballs; insert on antennae.

For head cupcake, trim and slightly bend antennae as needed and insert in cupcake. Position gumball eyes and nose. Pipe tip 3 dot pupils. Position chocolate dots for mouth. Assemble cupcakes in caterpillar formation.

*Combine Violet with Rose for violet shown.

Princess Crown

PAN: Cookie Sheet
COLORS:* Violet, Rose
FONDANT: White Ready-To-Use Rolled Fondant; Rolling Pin; Roll & Cut Mat; Brush Set; Bright Shimmer Dust™
RECIPE: Buttercream Icing, p. 101
ALSO: Crown Pattern, p. 115; Pastel Silicone Baking Cups; Spatula; sharp knife

See "Wilton Products", p. 118-127 for most Wilton items used in this project.

In advance: Make fondant crowns. Tint fondant light rose; also tint a 1/2 in. ball of dark violet and dark rose for each crown. Roll out light rose fondant 1/8 in. thick, position pattern and cut with knife. Stand crown on bottom edge; attach ends with damp brush. Roll tiny balls of dark violet and light rose fondant for "jewels"; attach to crown with damp brush. Let dry for at least 2 hours, then lightly brush entire crown with damp brush and sprinkle with Shimmer Dust; shake off excess.

Bake and cool cupcakes in silicone cups supported by cookie sheet. Ice smooth with spatula and position crown.

*Combine Violet with Rose for violet shown.

Pink Palace >

PANS: Mini Tasty-Fill; Standard Muffin
TIPS: 3, 18
COLORS: Rose, Red-Red
FONDANT: White Ready-To-Use Rolled Fondant; Heart Cut-Outs™; Rolling Pin; Roll & Cut Mat
RECIPES: Buttercream, Strawberry Buttercream, Royal Icings, p. 101
ALSO: Door, Window Patterns, p. 115; 8 in. Cake Circles; Meringue Powder; Cake Release; Pastry Brush; Spatula; peppermint sticks, waxed paper, toothpick, cornstarch

See "Wilton Products", p. 118-127 for most Wilton items used in this project.

In advance: Using royal icing on waxed paper-covered board, pipe tip 18 swirl spires, from 1 1/4 in. to 2 in. high. Let dry. **Also:** Make hearts. Tint portions of fondant red and rose. Roll out 1/8 in. thick. Cut hearts using smallest Cut-Outs. Let dry on cornstarch-dusted cake board.

Prepare pans with Cake Release. Bake and cool a cupcake without baking cup and 2-layer mini cake following package directions. Fill mini cake with strawberry buttercream; stack. Ice cakes smooth; position cupcake upside down on mini cake. Trace door and window patterns with toothpick, marking 4 medium windows on mini cake and 1 small window on cupcake. Outline and pipe in door and windows with tip 3 (smooth with finger dipped in cornstarch). Add tip 3 ball border around front door and dot doorknob. Pipe tip 3 ball top borders. Insert heart Cut-Outs into top borders, alternating colors. Cut 5 peppermint sticks to 4 in.; position around mini cake. Cut 2 sticks to 5 in.; insert in cupcake. Attach swirl spires to peppermint sticks with royal icing; let dry.

Enchanted Carriage

PAN: Jumbo Muffin
TIPS: 3, 6
COLORS: Lemon Yellow, Rose, Red-Red, Copper (skin tone)
FONDANT: White Ready-To-Use Rolled Fondant; Round, Heart Cut-Outs™; Rolling Pin; Roll & Cut Mat
RECIPES: Buttercream, Royal Icings, p. 101
ALSO: White Jumbo Baking Cups; Fine Tip Neon Colors FoodWriter™ Edible Color Markers; Meringue Powder; Parchment Triangles; Cake Board; Spatula; waxed paper, cornstarch

See "Wilton Products", p. 118-127 for most Wilton items used in this project.

In advance: Make wheels and heart trims. Tint portions of fondant light rose and red; roll out 1/8 in. thick. Using medium Cut-Outs, cut 2 round wheels and 1 heart roof topper for each treat. Using smallest Cut-Out, cut 3 heart door and window trims for each treat. Let dry on waxed paper-covered board dusted with cornstarch. **Also:** Make a 1 in. diameter puddle face (p. 111) using thinned royal icing in cut parchment bag. Let dry. Using full-strength royal icing, pipe tip 3 swirl hair and pull-out crown. Pipe tip 3 spirals on wheels. Draw facial features with black FoodWriter.

Ice cupcakes smooth in buttercream. Pipe tip 6 outline windows, carriage trim and door; pipe in tip 6 windows (smooth with finger dipped in cornstarch). Position face. Attach wheels and heart trims with icing.

Princess Takes a Dip

PANS: Standard Muffin; Non-Stick Cookie Sheet; Cooling Grid
TIPS: 2, 3
COLORS:* Rose, Brown, Red-Red, Copper (skin tone), Violet
FONDANT: White Ready-To-Use Rolled Fondant; Rolling Pin; Roll & Cut Mat; Round Cut-Outs™; Brush Set
RECIPES: Buttercream, Royal Icings, p. 101; favorite crisped rice cereal treats
ALSO: Crown Pattern, p. 115; Candy Melts®† in White and Pink; 4 in. Lollipop Sticks; Fine Tip Neon Colors FoodWriter™ Edible Color Markers; Gum-Tex™; Meringue Powder; Spatula; cake ice cream cones, paring knife, toothpick, waxed paper

See "Wilton Products", p. 118-127 for most Wilton items used in this project.

In advance: Make dress, girl, cone base and crown (p. 111). Place cones in muffin pan cavities. Bake and cool cupcakes in cones; trim top level with cone. Ice smooth in buttercream. Attach girl to cone and cone to cone base with melted candy; let set.

* Combine Brown with Red-Red for brown shown.
† Brand confectionery coating.

< Give Her an "A"!

PANS: Standard Muffin; Mini Muffin
TIPS: 3, 5, 127, 233
COLORS:* Copper (skin tone), Violet, Rose, Black
CANDY: White Candy Melts®†; Primary Candy Color Set
RECIPE: Buttercream Icing, p. 101
ALSO: Hair, Shoe Patterns, p. 115; White Standard, Mini Baking Cups; Cake Board; Spatula; waxed paper, cornstarch

See "Wilton Products", p. 118-127 for most Wilton items used in this project.

In advance: Make hair and shoes. Tape patterns to board (reverse shoe pattern to make right and left shoes); cover with waxed paper. Tint portion of melted white candy yellow using candy color. Pipe in patterns with melted candy; refrigerate until firm.

Ice smooth 2 standard and 6 mini cupcakes. Position on cake board. Attach hair and shoes with dots of icing. Pipe tip 3 outline eyes and tip 5 dot nose and cheeks (flatten and smooth with finger dipped in cornstarch). Pipe in tip 3 mouth, zigzag collar and sleeve trim. Pipe tip 127 ruffle skirt. Add tip 5 letter, zigzag socks and outline shoelaces. Pipe tip 3 pull-out puffs on shoes. Pipe tip 233 pull-out pompoms in alternating colors.

* Combine Violet with Rose for violet shown.

Purse-onal Treats >

PAN: 9 x 13 in. Sheet
COLORS:* Violet, Rose, Lemon Yellow
FONDANT: White Ready-To-Use Rolled Fondant; Rolling Pin; Roll & Cut Mat; Brush Set
RECIPE: Buttercream Icing, p. 101
ALSO: Round Comfort Grip™ Cutter; Fine Tip Neon Colors FoodWriter™ Edible Color Markers; White Candy Melts®†; 4 in. Lollipop Sticks; Nesting Heart Plastic Cutter Set; Cake Board; Gum-Tex™; Spatula; waxed paper, cornstarch, ruler

See "Wilton Products", p. 118-127 for most Wilton items used in this project.

Two days in advance: Make purse handles (p. 112). Let dry 48 hours on cornstarch-dusted board, in a cool, dark place. For clasps, roll two 3/8 in. balls each in yellow and violet. Reserve remaining tinted fondant.

Bake and cool sheet cake using firm-textured batter such as pound cake. Trim cake to 1 1/2 in. high. Cut circles using round cutter; trim 1/2 in. off one edge to create a straight bottom. Ice cakes smooth. Roll out fondant colors 1/8 in. thick. Cover cakes. For rose purse flap, cut a wedge of fondant and roll a small ball for snap; attach with damp brush. For violet and yellow purses, imprint seam for top opening with round end of brush. Using FoodWriters, draw dots, lines and spirals. Using purses as a guide, position handles; cut ends on an angle to conform to curve and adjust handle shapes as needed. Attach handles and clasps with damp brush.

* Combine Violet with Rose for violet shown.

Merry-Go-Round Centerpiece

PAN: Jumbo Muffin, Cookie Sheet, Cooling Grid
TIPS: 3, 16
COLORS: Violet, Rose
RECIPES: Buttercream, Color Flow Icings, p. 101; Roll-Out Cookie, p. 103
ALSO: White Jumbo Baking Cups; Animal Pals 50-Pc. Cutter Set; 8 in. Cookie Treat Sticks; Color Flow Mix; White Candy Melts®†; Heart Drops; Spatula; yellow curling ribbon, waxed paper, large spice drops

See "Wilton Products", p. 118-127 for most Wilton items used in this project.

In advance: Roll out dough; cut cookies using horse cutter. Using full-strength color flow, outline with tip 3; let set. Flow in with thinned color flow; let dry. Place cookies on waxed paper. In full-strength color flow, pipe tip 3 outline harness, dot nose and eyes, swirl mane and outline tail. Outline and pipe in tip 3 saddle and pipe in hooves. Wrap curling ribbon around cookie stick; secure with melted candy. Attach horse cookie to stick with melted candy; let set. Insert spice drop on top of stick.

Ice cupcakes smooth; insert stick. Pipe tip 16 rosettes around edge; position candy hearts.

† Brand confectionery coating.

American Beauties

PAN: Standard Muffin
TIPS: 2A, 126
COLORS:* Violet, Rose, Lemon Yellow
RECIPE: Buttercream Icing, p. 101
ALSO: White Standard Baking Cups; Cupcakes 'N More® Dessert Stand (holds 13); Spatula

See "Wilton Products", p. 118-127 for most Wilton items used in this project.

Ice cupcakes smooth. On each cupcake top, make a tip 126 rose with tip 2A base. Position cupcakes on stand.

*Combine Violet with Rose for violet shown.

‹Mixed Bouquet

PAN: Standard Muffin
TIPS: 3, 126, 352
COLORS*: Violet, Rose, Kelly Green, Lemon Yellow
RECIPE: Buttercream Icing, p. 101
ALSO: White, Assorted Pastel Standard Baking Cups; White, Yellow Sparkling Sugar

See "Wilton Products", p. 118-127 for most Wilton items used in this project.

Ice cupcakes smooth. For daisies, pipe tip 126 petals from cupcake edge to center. Pipe tip 3 ball center; sprinkle with yellow sugar. For rosebuds, pipe tip 126 half rose; add 2 side petals. Pipe tip 3 sepal and calyx; add tip 352 leaf. For apple blossom, pipe tip 126 apple blossom with tip 3 ball center; sprinkle center with white sugar.

*Combine Violet with Rose for violet shown.

Freshly Picked›

PAN: Standard Muffin
TIPS: 3, 349
COLORS:* Rose, Kelly Green, Violet, Lemon Yellow
FONDANT: White Ready-To-Use Rolled Fondant; Flower Cut-Outs™; Rolling Pin; Roll & Cut Mat
RECIPE: Buttercream Icing, p. 101
ALSO: White Standard Baking Cups

See "Wilton Products", p. 118-127 for most Wilton items used in this project.

In advance: Make small fondant flowers. Tint portions of fondant violet, rose and yellow. Roll out 1/8 in. thick; cut flowers using smallest Cut-Out. Set aside.

Ice cupcakes smooth. Tint remaining fondant light rose, light green, light violet and light yellow. Roll out 1/8 in. thick; cut flower backgrounds using largest Cut-Out. Position on cupcakes. Position small flowers. Pipe tip 3 outline stem and dot flower center. Add tip 349 leaves.

*Combine Violet with Rose for violet shown.

‹ Home Tweet Home

PANS: Jumbo Muffin; Cookie Sheet; Cooling Grid
TIPS: 1, 2, 5, 8, 131, 225, 349, 352
COLORS: Rose, Lemon Yellow, Kelly Green, Royal Blue, Violet, Black
RECIPES: Buttercream, Royal Icings, p. 101; Roll-Out Cookie, p. 103
ALSO: Roof Eaves Pattern, p. 115; White Jumbo Baking Cups; Square Cut-Outs™; 6 in. Cookie Treat Sticks; Meringue Powder; Cake Board; Rolling Pin; Disposable Decorating Bags; Spatula; waxed paper, cornstarch

See "Wilton Products", p. 118-127 for most Wilton items used in this project.

Two days in advance: Make eaves (p. 112). Make extras to allow for breakage and let dry 48 hours. **Also:** Make flowers, bluebird and heart window on waxed paper using royal icing. For each cupcake, pipe 7 tip 225 and 5 tip 131 drop flowers in yellow and rose. Add tip 2 dot centers in white. For bluebird, pipe tip 8 ball body and head (flatten and smooth with finger dipped in cornstarch). Pipe tip 352 pull-out wings. Add tip 2 pull-out beak and tip 1 dot eyes. For heart window, pipe tip 5 beads. Make extras of all and let dry.

Roll out cookie dough; cut birdhouse cookies using largest square Cut-Out. Using pattern, cut top of cookie into a peak. Bake and cool. Outline cookies using tip 2 and royal icing. Flow in with thinned royal icing in cut bag; let dry. Cut stick to 5¹/₂ in.; attach cookie with full-strength royal icing. Attach bluebird, heart window and eaves. Attach flowers and pipe tip 349 leaves on eaves. Ice cupcakes smooth in buttercream. Insert stick. Position flowers on cupcake. Add tip 349 leaves.

Pick to Click ›

PANS: Cookie Sheet; Cooling Grid
TIPS: 2, 8
COLORS: Rose, Lemon Yellow, Violet
RECIPES: Buttercream, Color Flow Icings, p. 101; Roll-Out Cookie, p. 103
ALSO: Pastel Silicone Baking Cups; Flower Cut-Outs™; 4 in. Lollipop Sticks; Green Cake Sparkles™; Color Flow Mix Icing; Rolling Pin; Parchment Triangles; Spatula; waxed paper, jelly spearmint leaves

See "Wilton Products", p. 118-127 for most Wilton items used in this project.

One day in advance: Make cookies. Roll out dough; cut cookies using medium Flower Cut-Out. Bake and cool. Outline cookies with tip 2 and full-strength Color Flow. Flow in with thinned color flow in cut parchment bag. Let dry overnight. Attach cookies to sticks with full-strength color flow. Pipe tip 8 dot flower center in buttercream.

Bake and cool cupcakes in silicone cups supported by cookie sheet. Ice smooth; sprinkle with Cake Sparkles. Insert cookies on sticks. Cut spearmint leaves in half and attach to stem with icing.

<Party Petals

PAN:	Cookie Sheet
TIPS:	3, 5
COLORS:	Lemon Yellow, Rose, Royal Blue, Black
RECIPES:	Buttercream, Royal Icings, p. 101
ALSO:	Loop Petal Pattern, p. 115; Pastel Silicone Baking Cups; Meringue Powder; Cake Board; Spatula; waxed paper, cornstarch

See "Wilton Products", p. 118-127 for most Wilton items used in this project.

In advance: Make petals in royal icing (approximately 25 for each flower). Tape pattern to board; cover with waxed paper. Outline petals with tip 5. Make extras to allow for breakage and let dry overnight.

Bake and cool cupcakes in silicone cups supported by cookie sheet. Ice smooth in buttercream, building up to a $1/2$ in. rounded layer. Pipe tip 3 dot eyes and string mouth; add tip 3 dot cheeks (flatten and smooth with finger dipped in cornstarch). Insert loops in overlapping fashion.

Gathering Flowers >

PAN:	Cookie Sheet
TIPS:	3, 349
COLORS:	Kelly Green, Violet, Rose, Lemon Yellow, Royal Blue
RECIPE:	Buttercream Icing, p. 101
FONDANT:	White Ready-To-Use Rolled Fondant; Flower Cut-Outs™; Rolling Pin; Roll & Cut Mat
ALSO:	Pastel Silicone Baking Cups; Cake Boards; Spatula; waxed paper, cornstarch

See "Wilton Products", p. 118-127 for most Wilton items used in this project.

In advance: Make flowers. Tint portions of fondant yellow, rose and blue; roll out $1/8$ in. thick. Using smallest flower cutter, cut out approximately 12 flowers for each cupcake; let dry on cornstarch-dusted board. Pipe tip 3 dot centers; let dry.

Bake and cool cupcakes in silicone cups supported by cookie sheet. Ice smooth. Pipe tip 3 stems; position flowers. Add tip 349 leaves. Pipe tip 3 string bow.

It's Always Cupcake Season!

Your cupcake pans may never take a holiday—because these days, cupcakes are served at celebrations for every season. They're welcome anytime, whether carried to a summer BBQ or displayed as a Christmas centerpiece.

Wait until you see the fun new ways we're decorating for every time of year! Now you can create amazing displays, like the winter scene here, with cute cookie skiers and sugar cone Christmas trees. Cupcake shapes have changed too. With our colorful silicone baking cups, round is just one of your options. Look for pretty Easter baskets in square cups, Valentine love notes in hearts and an adorable Christmas angel in a triangle cup.

Shown: *Skier's Spree*; instructions, p. 94.

‹ Fun Beneath a Wreath

PAN: Cookie Sheet
TIP: 3
RECIPE: Buttercream Icing, p. 101
ALSO: Christmas Silicone Baking Cups; Jumbo Nonpareils Sprinkle Decorations; Rolling Pin; spearmint jelly leaves, red spice drops, waxed paper, granulated sugar, scissors, paring knife

See "Wilton Products", p. 118-127 for most Wilton items used in this project.

Bake and cool cupcakes in silicone cups supported by cookie sheet. Ice smooth. Roll out spice drops on waxed paper sprinkled with sugar. Cut triangle shapes for bow and dot shape for knot. Cut spearmint leaves in strips; position upright or angled on cupcake. Attach bow with tip 3 dots of icing. Position nonpareils on leaves.

‹ Holiday's First Flower

PAN: Standard Muffin
TIP: 6
COLORS: Kelly Green, Lemon Yellow
RECIPE: Buttercream Icing, p. 101
ALSO: White Standard Baking Cups; 6-Mix Christmas Sprinkle Assortment; Leaf Cut-Outs™; Rolling Pin; red spice drops, granulated sugar, waxed paper

See "Wilton Products", p. 118-127 for most Wilton items used in this project.

Ice cupcakes smooth. Roll out spice drops on waxed paper sprinkled with sugar. Cut 6 petals each using medium and small Leaf Cut-Outs for each cupcake. Position petals. Pipe a tip 6 ball for flower center; position nonpareils.

Show Off Your Fir ›

PAN: Cookie Sheet
TIP: 16
COLOR: Kelly Green
RECIPE: Buttercream Icing, p. 101
ALSO: Triangle Silicone Baking Cups; Jumbo Stars Sprinkle Decorations, Jumbo Nonpareils Sprinkle Decorations; confectioner's sugar

See "Wilton Products", p. 118-127 for most Wilton items used in this project.

Bake and cool cupcakes in silicone cups supported by cookie sheet. Cover with tip 16 pull-out star leaves. Position star sprinkle on treetop; position nonpareils on leaves. Sprinkle with confectioner's sugar.

‹ Candy Cane

PAN: Standard Muffin
TIP: 1M (2110)
RECIPE: Buttercream Icing, p. 101
ALSO: White Standard Baking Cups; Red Color Mist™; White Sparkling Sugar; Red Cake Sparkles™

See "Wilton Products", p. 118-127 for most Wilton items used in this project.

Cover cupcakes with tip 1M swirl. Spray half of cupcakes with Color Mist; sprinkle with red Cake Sparkles. Sprinkle white cupcakes with white Sparkling Sugar. Position in candy cane formation.

Happy Holly Days ⌄

PANS: Standard Muffin, Cookie Sheet, Cooling Grid
COLOR: Kelly Green
RECIPES: Buttercream Icing, p. 101; Roll-Out Cookie, p. 103
ALSO: Silver Foil Standard Baking Cups; Holiday Mini Cutter Set; Dark Green Colored Sugar; Rolling Pin; Cutter/Embosser; red candy-coated chocolate dots

See "Wilton Products", p. 118-127 for most Wilton items used in this project.

Tint cookie dough green. Roll out and cut leaves with Mini Cutter; score vein lines with straight-edge wheel of Cutter/Embosser. Sprinkle with sugar; bake and cool. Ice cupcakes smooth. Position leaves and chocolate dot berries.

Pinwheel Mint ›

PAN: Standard Muffin
FONDANT: White Ready-To-Use Rolled Fondant; Primary Colors Fondant Multi Pack; Rolling Pin; Roll & Cut Mat; Brush Set
RECIPES: Buttercream Icing, p. 101; Thinned Fondant Adhesive, p. 102
ALSO: White Standard Baking Cups; Gum-Tex™; 4 in. Lollipop Sticks; Cake Board; paring knife, cornstarch

See "Wilton Products", p. 118-127 for most Wilton items used in this project.

In advance: Make wrapper ends. Add ½ teaspoon Gum-Tex to 6 oz. white fondant. Roll out ⅛ in. thick; cut two 1 x 3 in. long strips. Ruffle strips by folding in thirds; pinch end. Let dry on cornstarch-dusted cake board. Cut lollipop sticks to 2½ in.; attach wrapper end to lollipop stick with fondant adhesive, leaving 1½ in. extended. Let dry.

Ice cupcakes smooth. For mint spirals, roll out red fondant ⅛ in. thick. Cut three 1½ x ⅛ in. strips and three 1½ x ½ in. strips that taper to ¼ in. wide. Position on cupcake in swirl formation. Roll a ¼ in. dot; attach at center with damp brush. Insert wrapper ends in cupcake.

< A Giving Guy

PAN:	Cookie Sheet
TIPS:	2, 3, 16
COLORS:	Red-Red, Copper (skin tone), Black
FONDANT:	White Ready-To-Use Rolled Fondant; Rolling Pin; Roll & Cut Mat; Brush Set
RECIPE:	Buttercream Icing, p. 101
ALSO:	Silicone Baking Cups; Cake Board

See "Wilton Products", p. 118-127 for most Wilton items used in this project.

Bake and cool cupcakes in silicone cups supported by cookie sheet. Ice smooth in copper; place on cake board. For hat, tint a 2 in. ball of fondant red; roll into a tapered log 6 in. long. Flatten log slightly at wider end. Shape into a curve and position on cupcake top, extending tapered end on board. Pipe tip 16 swirl beard. Pipe tip 2 outline eyes and eyebrows; pipe in mouth. Add tip 16 pull-out star moustache; pipe tip 3 dot nose. Pipe tip 3 swirl hat brim. For pompom, roll a 3/4 in. fondant ball. Indent slightly with end of brush; attach to hat with damp brush.

< Deer Friend

PAN:	Cookie Sheet
TIP:	3
COLOR:	Black
RECIPES:	Buttercream, Chocolate Buttercream Icings, p. 101
ALSO:	Antler Patterns, p. 115; Silicone Baking Cups; Light Cocoa Candy Melts®†; Parchment Paper; Cake Boards; black jelly beans, waxed paper

See "Wilton Products", p. 118-127 for most Wilton items used in this project.

In advance: Make antlers. Trace patterns on parchment paper; tape to cake boards and cover with waxed paper. Using melted candy in cut parchment bag, pipe in antlers; refrigerate until firm.

Bake and cool cupcakes in silicone cups supported by cookie sheet; ice smooth. Insert antlers. Pipe tip 3 ball eyes and dot pupils. Position jelly bean nose. Pipe tip 3 outline mouth.

† Brand confectionery coating.

< Penguin Party

PAN:	Cookie Sheet
TIPS:	3, 4
COLORS:	Black, Red-Red
FONDANT:	White Ready-To-Use Rolled Fondant; Rolling Pin; Roll & Cut Mat; Brush Set
RECIPES:	Buttercream Icing, p. 101; Thinned Fondant Adhesive, p. 102
ALSO:	Penguin Face, Hat Patterns, p. 115; Silicone Baking Cups; 4 in. Lollipop Sticks; Chocolate Ready-To-Use Decorator Icing; Cake Board; waxed paper, cornstarch, toothpicks, candy corn, jelly fruit slices, paring knife, toothpick

See "Wilton Products", p. 118-127 for most Wilton items used in this project.

In advance: Make hat. Tint 1 oz. fondant red. Roll out 1/8 in. thick; trace pattern with toothpick and cut out. Let dry on cornstarch-dusted cake board. Cut a lollipop stick to 3 in. long. Attach to back of hat with fondant adhesive, leaving 1 1/2 in. extended at bottom.

Bake and cool cupcakes in silicone cups supported by cookie sheet. Ice cupcakes smooth in white. Mark face pattern with toothpick. Tint chocolate icing black. Using tip 4, pipe in outer area (smooth with finger dipped in cornstarch). Pipe tip 3 dot eyes. Cut fruit slice in half and position for feet. Insert hat and candy corn nose. Shape 3/8 in. wide fondant hat brim and 1/4 in. ball pompom. Attach with fondant adhesive. Imprint brim with dots using toothpick.

‹ A Place to Chill

PANS: Mini Ball; Cookie Sheet; Cooling Grid
TIP: 3
COLORS: Black, Red-Red, Golden Yellow
RECIPES: Buttercream, Royal Icings, p. 101; Roll-Out Cookie, p. 103
ALSO: Holiday Mini Cutter Set; Meringue Powder; Cake Circle; 4 in. Lollipop Sticks; Rolling Pin; marshmallows, paring knife, waxed paper

See "Wilton Products", p. 118-127 for most Wilton items used in this project.

In advance: Make cookies. Roll out dough; cut penguins using gingerbread boy cutter from set. Cut easels using Christmas tree cutter; cut vertically in half to make 2 and cut bottom level. Bake and cool. Place penguins on waxed paper. Pipe in penguin bodies and hats with tip 3 and royal icing. Pipe tip 3 pull-out beak and wings, bead feet, dot eyes and zigzag hat trim; let dry. Attach easels to back with royal icing; let dry.

Ice mini ball cakes smooth in buttercream; score brick lines with lollipop stick. Cut marshmallow in half, angling back to conform to curve of mini ball. Attach to cake with dots of icing. Position penguin.

Snow Drifters ›

PAN: Cookie Sheet
TIP: 3
COLORS: * Red-Red, Kelly Green, Black, Orange, Violet, Rose
FONDANT: White Ready-To-Use Rolled Fondant; Rolling Pin; Roll & Cut Mat; Round Cut-Outs™; Brush Set
RECIPES: Buttercream Icing, p. 101; Thinned Fondant Adhesive, p. 102
ALSO: Hat, Vest Patterns, p. 116; Silicone Baking Cups; Tapered Spatula; Cake Board; 6 in. Lollipop Sticks; cornstarch, waxed paper, toothpick, paring knife

See "Wilton Products", p. 118-127 for most Wilton items used in this project.

In advance: Make hats, mittens and heads. Tint portions of fondant red and green; roll out 1/8 in. thick. Trace hat patterns with toothpick and cut out with knife. Shape flattened balls for mittens, 3/4 in. diameter; cut a notch for thumb. Roll out white fondant 1/8 in. thick; cut heads using medium Round Cut-Out. Tint small amounts of white fondant black, orange and violet. Roll small balls for eyes, a 3/8 in. cone for nose and a 1/8 x 1/2 in. log for mouth; attach facial features and hats with fondant adhesive. Cut a 1/8 in. wide strip for hat band; attach. Reserve violet fondant.

Bake and cool cupcakes in silicone cups supported by cookie sheet; ice smooth. Pipe tip 3 swirl hat brim and pompom. For each snowman, cut one lollipop stick to 3 in. and two sticks to 2 1/2 in.; attach heads to 3 in. sticks with icing and insert in cupcakes. Insert mittens on 2 1/2 in. sticks; insert in cupcakes. Roll out green and red fondant to 1/8 in. thick. Trace vest pattern; cut out and position on cupcake. Pipe tip 3 dots in buttercream. Cut three 1/4 x 1 1/2 in. fondant strips for scarf; wrap around neck. Shape 3/4 in. fondant triangles in violet for bow tie and a 1/4 in. ball for knot; attach. Shape 3/8 in. ball buttons; position on cupcakes.

*Combine Violet with Rose for violet shown.

‹ Tree Toppers

PAN: Cookie Sheet
COLOR: Kelly Green
FONDANT: White Ready-To-Use Rolled Fondant; Rolling Pin; Roll & Cut Mat
RECIPE: Buttercream Icing, p. 101; Thinned Fondant Adhesive, p. 102
ALSO: Pastel Silicone Baking Cups; Jumbo Stars Sprinkle Decorations; 4 in. Lollipop Sticks; Fine Tip, Primary Colors FoodWriter™ Edible Color Markers; 18-Pc. Holiday Metal Cutter Set; White Sparkling Sugar; Gum-Tex™; Cake Board; cornstarch

See "Wilton Products", p. 118-127 for most Wilton items used in this project.

Several days in advance: Make trees. Add 1 teaspoon Gum-Tex to 12 oz. white fondant (for approximately 24-30 trees); tint green. Roll out 1/8 in. thick. Cut trees using cookie cutter. Let dry on cornstarch-dusted cake board. Draw tree branches with green FoodWriter. Attach lollipop stick to back of tree with fondant adhesive, leaving 1¹/₂ in. extended at base.

Bake and cool cupcakes in silicone cups supported by cookie sheet. Ice smooth; sprinkle with sugar. Attach star sprinkle to tree with icing. Insert tree in cupcake.

Hang On For Treats! ›

PANS: Cookie Sheet
TIPS: 2, 4, 45
COLORS:* Violet, Sky Blue, Rose, Kelly Green
RECIPES: Royal, Buttercream Icings, p. 101
ALSO: Ornament Hanger Pattern, p. 115; Silicone Baking Cups; Meringue Powder; large marshmallows, waxed paper, cornstarch, paring knife, toothpick

See "Wilton Products", p. 118-127 for most Wilton items used in this project.

In advance: Make hangers. Cover pattern with waxed paper; pipe tip 4 hangers using royal icing. Let dry overnight.

Bake and cool cupcakes in silicone cups supported by cookie sheet. For snowflake ornaments, ice smooth in buttercream. Pipe tip 2 string snowflakes; pipe tip 2 dots at center and snowflake points and randomly between flakes. For diamond ornaments, ice smooth. Mark diamond shape with tooth pick. Pipe in diamond with tip 4 (smooth with finger dipped in cornstarch). Outline diamond with tip 2. Pipe tip 45 band across cupcake; pipe tip 2 dots on band. Cut marshmallow in half; cut a small hole in marshmallow center. Insert hanger. Press marshmallow against side of baking cup, securing with icing if needed.

*Combine Violet with Rose for violet shown.

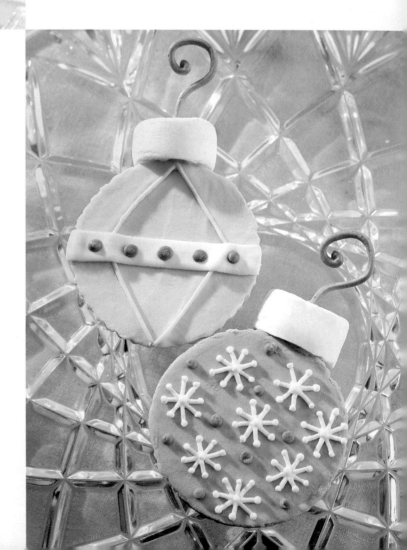

‹Holiday Angel

PAN: Cookie Sheet

TIPS: 2, 3, 4, 12

COLORS: Lemon Yellow, Copper (skin tone), Brown, Black

RECIPE: Buttercream Icing, p. 101

ALSO: Triangle Silicone Baking Cups; Nesting Hearts Cutter Set; 101 Cookie Cutters Set; White Ready-To-Use Rolled Fondant; White Cake Sparkles™; Brush Set; Rolling Pin; Roll & Cut Mat; Piping Gel; 4 in. Lollipop Sticks; Cake Board; waxed paper, cornstarch, paring knife, scissors, ruler

See "Wilton Products", p. 118-127 for most Wilton items used in this project.

At least one day in advance: Make wings. Roll out white fondant 1/8 in. thick. Cut heart shape using 2 1/2 in. cutter; cut heart in half with paring knife. Let dry on waxed paper-covered board dusted with cornstarch. Brush halves with piping gel; sprinkle with sparkles. Let dry. **Also:** Make face and halo. Tint portions of fondant copper and yellow; roll out 1/8 in. thick. Using smallest circle cutter from set, cut a circle for face; cut a cresecent shape for halo. Let dry on waxed paper-covered board dusted with cornstarch.

Bake and cool cupcakes in silicone cups supported by cookie sheet. Ice smooth in buttercream. Cut lollipop stick to 3 in.; insert horizontally through top of cupcake. Position and attach wings to stick with icing. Attach head and halo with icing; let dry. Pipe tip 3 swirl hair and dot nose, tip 2 dot eyes and string mouth. Add tip 12 arms and tip 4 outline hands.

Season's Sparkle! ›

PAN: Standard Muffin

TIP: 2

COLOR: Royal Blue

RECIPES: Buttercream, Royal Icings, p. 101

ALSO: Snowflake Pattern, p. 116; Cupcake Pedestals; Silver Foil Standard Baking Cups; Cake Board; Meringue Powder; waxed paper, vegetable oil pan spray, cellophane tape, paring knife, sheet of paper

See "Wilton Products", p. 118-127 for most Wilton items used in this project.

Two days in advance: Make royal icing snowflakes. Tape pattern to board; cover with waxed paper. Spray lightly with pan spray; wipe off excess. Pipe snowflake with tip 2 lines and dots, using royal icing and heavy pressure. Let dry overnight. Gently slide piece of paper under snowflakes to loosen. Carefully turn over snowflake and overpipe with tip 2. Let dry overnight.

Ice cupcakes smooth in buttercream. With knife, cut a small hole in cupcake top; insert snowflake. Position cupcakes on pedestals.

‹Ripe for Romance

PAN: Cookie Sheet
CANDY: Light Cocoa Candy Melts®†; Decorator Brush Set
ALSO: Heart Silicone Baking Cups; fresh raspberries, blueberries
See "Wilton Products", p. 118-127 for most Wilton items used in this project.

Place baking cups on cookie sheet. Fill cups with 2 tablespoons melted candy; brush candy up sides, coating evenly to make heart candy shell (p. 113). Refrigerate until firm. Peel cup off candy, gently pushing up shell from bottom. Fill with fruit.

† Brand confectionery coating.

Sweetly Stated ›

PAN: Cookie Sheet
TIP: 3
COLORS:* Lemon Yellow, Golden Yellow, Red-Red, Christmas Red, Kelly Green, Rose
RECIPE: Buttercream Icing, p. 101
ALSO: Heart Silicone Baking Cups
See "Wilton Products", p. 118-127 for most Wilton items used in this project.

Bake and cool cupcakes in silicone cups supported by cookie sheet. Ice smooth. Print tip 3 message.

*Combine Lemon Yellow with Golden Yellow for yellow shown. Combine Red-Red with Christmas Red for red shown.

⌃ Cubby Love

PAN: Standard Muffin

TIPS: 1, 2A, 3, 12

COLORS:* Rose, Black, Brown, Red-Red

FONDANT: White Ready-To-Use Rolled Fondant; Rolling Pin; Roll & Cut Mat

RECIPE: Buttercream Icing, p. 101

ALSO: Nesting Hearts Plastic Cutter Set; Hearts Standard Baking Cups; Gum-Tex™; Fine Tip Primary Colors FoodWriter™ Edible Color Markers; cornstarch

See "Wilton Products", p. 118-127 for most Wilton items used in this project.

In advance: Make hearts. Add ⅛ teaspoon Gum-Tex to a 2 in. ball of fondant; tint rose. Roll out ⅛ in. thick; cut hearts using 2nd smallest cutter. Let dry. Write message using red FoodWriter.

Ice cupcakes smooth. Figure pipe bear on cupcake using tips 2A, 12, 3 and 1 (p. 110).

* Combine Brown with Red-Red for brown shown.

⌃ Amorous Archery

PAN: Cookie Sheet

TIPS: 3, 18

COLOR: Rose

CANDY: Candy Melts®† in Red and White; Hearts Candy Mold; Deep Heart Truffle Candy Mold; Garden Candy Color Set

RECIPE: Buttercream Icing, p. 101

ALSO: Heart Silicone Baking Cups; Red Colored Sugar; 6 in. Cookie Treat Sticks

See "Wilton Products", p. 118-127 for most Wilton items used in this project.

In advance: Make candy heart. Fill truffle mold cavity halfway with melted red candy; refrigerate until firm. Tint portion of white candy light pink using candy color; pour into Hearts Mold cavities. Refrigerate until firm. Cut sticks to 5½ in.; attach smaller hearts with melted candy.

Bake and cool cupcakes in silicone molds supported by cookie sheet. Cover tops with tip 18 outlines, following heart shape and working from outer edge

to center. Sprinkle cupcake with sugar. Position stick; add heart truffle. Pipe tip 3 pull-out feathers on end of stick; overpipe.

⌃ Sweet Reminders

PANS: Standard Muffin; Cookie Sheet; Cooling Grid

TIPS: 1M (2110), 3

COLOR: Rose

RECIPE: Buttercream Icing, Color Flow Icing, p. 101; Roll-Out Cookie, p. 103

ALSO: Nesting Hearts Cutter Set; Valentine Nonpareils Sprinkle Decorations; Hearts Standard Baking Cups; Color Flow Mix; Rolling Pin

See "Wilton Products", p. 118-127 for most Wilton items used in this project.

Roll out cookie dough. Cut cookies using 2nd smallest cutter; bake and cool. Outline with tip 3 using full-strength color flow; flow in with thinned color flow. Let dry. In buttercream, cover cupcakes with tip 1M swirl; sprinkle with nonpareils. Insert cookie in cupcake.

Bursting from Their Shells!

PANS: Standard Muffin; Cookie Sheet; Cooling Grid

TIP: 4

COLORS:* Lemon Yellow, Rose, Sky Blue, Violet, Leaf Green

RECIPES: Buttercream, Royal Icings, p. 101; Roll-Out Cookie, p. 103

ALSO: Cupcakes 'N More® Dessert Stand (holds 13); Bunnies & Chicks Standard Baking Cups; 4 in. Lollipop Sticks; Oval Cut-Outs™; Rolling Pin; Meringue Powder; shredded coconut, zip-close plastic bag

See "Wilton Products", p. 118-127 for most Wilton items used in this project.

In advance: Make cookies. Roll out cookie dough. Cut cookies using largest Oval Cut-Out; bake and cool. Place cookies on cooling grid over drip pan; cover with thinned royal icing. Let dry. Trim lollipop sticks to 2½ in.; attach to back of cookies with full-strength royal icing, leaving 1 in. extended. Let dry.

Tint remaining royal icing yellow, rose, blue and violet. Using tip 4, decorate cookies with dots and zigzags. Let dry.

Ice cupcakes smooth in buttercream. Tint coconut by placing in zip-close bag with a few drops of icing color; knead. Sprinkle tops with coconut; insert cookie. Position cupcakes on stand.

*Combine Violet with Rose for violet shown.

‹ Easter Buddies!

PAN:	Standard Muffin
COLORS:*	Lemon Yellow, Golden Yellow
CANDY:	Candy Melts®† in White, Yellow, Orange; Garden Candy Color Set
RECIPE:	Buttercream Icing, p. 101
ALSO:	Chick Beak, Hair, Wings, Feet Patterns, p. 116; Bunny Ears, Hands, Feet, Nose, Cheeks, Teeth Patterns, p. 116; Bunnies & Chicks Standard Baking Cups; Parchment Triangles; Cake Board; waxed paper

See "Wilton Products", p. 118-127 for most Wilton items used in this project.

In advance: Make candy trims. Tint portions of melted white candy pink and black using candy colors. Trace patterns on paper; tape onto cake board and cover with waxed paper. Using melted candy in cut parchment bags, pipe in patterns in colors shown; pipe black outline eyes for bunny and chick. Refrigerate until firm. Pipe in center of bunny ears and dot foot pads with pink candy; refrigerate until firm.

Ice cupcakes smooth. Position and insert candy, supporting with dots of icing if needed.

∗ Combine Lemon Yellow with Golden Yellow for yellow shown.
† Brand confectionery coating.

Care for a Carrot? ›

PANS:	Standard Muffin; Cookie Sheet; Cooling Grid
TIPS:	3, 9, 349
COLORS:	Rose, Kelly Green, Black
RECIPES:	Buttercream, Royal Icings, p. 101; Roll-Out Cookie, p. 103
ALSO:	Bunnies & Chicks Standard Baking Cups; 4 in. Lollipop Sticks; Nesting Bunnies Plastic Cutter Set; Rolling Pin; Meringue Powder; candy corn

See "Wilton Products", p. 118-127 for most Wilton items used in this project.

In advance: Make cookies. Roll out dough. Cut bunnies using smallest cutter; bake and cool. Place cookies on cooling grid over drip pan; cover with thinned royal icing. Let dry. Cut lollipop sticks to 2½ in.; attach to cookies with full-strength royal icing, leaving 1 in. extended at bottom. Let dry overnight.

Ice cupcakes smooth in buttercream. Finish bunnies with tip 3 dot eyes and nose, ball cheeks and outline inside ears. Insert in cupcake. Pipe tip 9 outline arms and dot thumbs. Insert candy corn. Pipe tip 349 pull-out leaves.

<Eggs in a Basket

PAN: Cookie Sheet
COLORS:* Lemon Yellow, Golden Yellow, Sky Blue, Leaf Green
ALSO: Pastel and Square Silicone Baking Cups; White Ready-To-Use Rolled Fondant; Jordan Almonds; Cake Board; shredded coconut, zip-close plastic bag, waxed paper, cornstarch

See "Wilton Products", p. 118-127 for most Wilton items used in this project.

One day in advance: Make basket handles. Add 1/2 teaspoon Gum-Tex to 8 oz. portion of fondant (for approximately 16 baskets); divide fondant in half and tint portions blue and yellow to match baking cups. Roll two 1/4 in. diameter logs; make fondant ropes (p. 113) in each color. Position ropes flat on waxed paper-covered board, forming an arch 2 in. high and 2 in. apart at the bottom; trim off excess. Let dry overnight.

Bake and cool cupcakes in silicone cups supported by cookie sheet. Ice smooth. Insert handles. Tint coconut by placing in zip-close bag with a few drops of icing color; knead. Position almonds and sprinkle with coconut.

*Combine Lemon Yellow with Golden Yellow for yellow shown.

Bonnet Season >

PAN: Standard Muffin
TIPS: 1, 2, 349
COLORS:* Lemon Yellow, Rose, Violet, Royal Blue, Leaf Green
FONDANT: White Ready-To-Use Rolled Fondant; Rolling Pin; Roll & Cut Mat; Cutter/Embosser; Brush Set
RECIPE: Buttercream Icing, p. 101
ALSO: White Standard Baking Cups; Floral Collection Flower Making Set; Blossom Nesting Metal Cutter Set; Cake Board; cornstarch

See "Wilton Products", p. 118-127 for most Wilton items used in this project.

In advance: Make fondant flowers. For every 3 cupcakes in colors shown, tint a 1 in. ball of fondant blue, 2 in. balls yellow, rose and violet. Roll out colors 1/8 in. thick. Using Flower Making Set cutters, cut 6 apple blossoms in violet and 12 forget-me-nots in rose. Place flowers on thick foam and cup centers using round stick from set. Let dry overnight on cornstarch-dusted board.

Ice cupcakes smooth. Roll out remaining fondant colors 1/8 in. thick. Cut blossom brims using 2nd smallest metal cutter; position on cupcake. Roll a matching color fondant ball, flatten to 1 1/2 in. wide x 3/4 in. high; attach in center of brim with damp brush. Cut blue hat bands, 1/4 x 5 1/2 in.; attach with damp brush. Outline brims with tip 1; add tip 1 dots at petal points. Attach flowers with dots of icing. Pipe tip 2 dot centers in buttercream. Pipe tip 349 leaves.

*Combine Violet wtih Rose for violet shown.

‹ Landing on His Feet!

PANS: Cookie Sheet; Cooling Grid
TIPS: 3, 46, 349
COLORS:* Lemon Yellow, Violet, Rose
RECIPES: Buttercream Icing, p. 101; Roll-Out Cookie, p. 103
ALSO: Silly-Feet™ Silicone Baking Cups; Round, Leaf Cut-Outs™; Fine Tip Primary Colors FoodWriter™ Edible Color Markers; Rolling Pin; 4 in. Lollipop Sticks; Parchment Triangles; spice drops, paring knife

See "Wilton Products", p. 118-127 for most Wilton items used in this project.

In advance: Make cookies. Tint dough yellow; roll out. Cut head and 2 wings using medium round and leaf Cut-Outs; reverse one leaf. Thin a portion of dough with water for piping. Pipe tip 349 hair tuft on heads and feathers on wings. Bake and cool. Cut lollipop sticks to 2 1/2 in.; attach to backs of cookies with dots of icing, leaving 1 1/2 in. extended.

Bake and cool cupcakes in Silly-Feet cups supported by cookie sheet. Mound icing, about 3/4 to 1 in. thick; smooth. Draw eyes with black FoodWriter. For beak, cut orange spice drop horizontally in half; cut a slit in top half for mouth and shape. Attach with icing. Pipe tip 46 (smooth side up) outline suspenders. Add tip 3 dot buttons. Insert head and wing cookies.

*Combine Violet with Rose for violet shown.

Shells in Pastels ›

PAN: Mini Egg
FONDANT: Pastel Colors Fondant Multi Pack; Fondant Ribbon Cutter/Embosser; Round Cut-Outs™; Rolling Pin; Roll & Cut Mat; Brush Set
RECIPE: Buttercream Icing, p. 101
ALSO: White Cake Sparkles; waxed paper, tea strainer

See "Wilton Products", p. 118-127 for most Wilton items used in this project.

Ice egg cakes smooth. Roll out fondant 1/8 in. thick. Cut some strips using straight-edge wheel of Ribbon Cutter/Embosser without spacers; cut other strips using zigzag-edge wheel without spacers. Cut dots using smallest Cut-Out. Brush all pieces with water and sprinkle with Cake Sparkles crushed through tea strainer. Position on cakes.

<Flag Festivities

PAN: Standard Muffin
RECIPE: Buttercream Icing, p. 101
ALSO: Old Glory Standard Baking Cups; Patriotic Flags Icing Decorations; Patriotic Mix Sprinkle Decorations; 4 in. Lollipop Sticks

See "Wilton Products", p. 118-127 for most Wilton items used in this project.

Ice cupcakes smooth; add sprinkles. Insert stick; trim as needed, leaving 2 in. extended. Attach icing decoration to lollipop stick using stiff buttercream.

Old Glory, New Look >

PAN: Standard Muffin
TIP: 8
COLORS:* Royal Blue, Red-Red, Christmas Red
FONDANT: White Ready-To-Use Rolled Fondant; Star Cut-Outs™; Rolling Pin; Roll & Cut Mat
RECIPE: Buttercream Icing, p. 101
ALSO: Old Glory Standard Baking Cups

See "Wilton Products", p. 118-127 for most Wilton items used in this project.

On cupcake tops, ice blue star background area smooth. Pipe tip 8 stripes in alternating colors. Roll out fondant 1/8 in. thick. Cut stars using smallest Cut-Out; position on cupcake.

*Combine Red-Red with Christmas Red for red shown.

‹ Sam's the Man

PAN: Standard Muffin; Cookie Sheet; Cooling Grid
TIPS: 2, 3, 4, 7
COLORS:* Red-Red, Christmas Red, Royal Blue, Black, Copper (skin tone)
RECIPES: Buttercream Icing, p. 101; Roll-Out Cookie, p. 103
ALSO: Uncle Sam Hat Pattern, p. 116; Patriotic Stars Standard Baking Cups; Rolling Pin; toothpick, paring knife, cornstarch, large marshmallows

See "Wilton Products", p. 118-127 for most Wilton items used in this project.

Roll out cookie dough. Trace hat pattern with toothpick; cut cookies with knife. Bake and cool. Ice brim area smooth. Pipe tip 7 hat band and alternating stripes (pat smooth with finger dipped in cornstarch). Ice cupcake smooth. Pipe tip 3 dot eyes, tip 2 dot pupils and tip 4 ball nose (pat all smooth with finger dipped in cornstarch). Outline and pipe in tip 2 mouth. With heavy pressure, pipe tip 4 outline hair, beard and moustache. Attach hat cookie with icing, supporting with marshmallow.

*Combine Red-Red with Christmas Red for red shown.

Shooting Stars ›

PAN: Standard Muffin; Cookie Sheet; Cooling Grid
COLORS:* Red-Red, Christmas Red, Royal Blue
RECIPES: Buttercream, Color Flow Icings, p. 101; Roll-Out Cookie, p. 103
ALSO: Patriotic Stars Standard Baking Cups; Star Cut-Outs™; Red and Blue Cake Sparkles™; 4 in. Lollipop Sticks; Color Flow Mix; Rolling Pin; red and blue curling ribbon, tea strainer, waxed paper

See "Wilton Products", p. 118-127 for most Wilton items used in this project.

One day in advance: Make cookies. Roll out dough. Cut star cookies using medium Cut-Out; bake and cool. Place cookies on cooling grid over drip pan; cover with thinned color flow. Let set for a few minutes; sprinkle with Cake Sparkles crushed through tea strainer. Let set overnight on waxed paper-covered surface. Attach lollipop sticks to cookies with full-strength color flow; let set.

Ice cupcakes smooth. Trim sticks for blue cookies to 2½ in., for red cookies trim to 3½ in. Insert cookies in cupcakes; tie curling ribbon to sticks.

*Combine Red-Red with Christmas Red for red shown.

<Putting Their Heads Together

PANS:	Standard; Mini Muffin
COLOR:	Orange
CANDY:	Yellow Candy Melts®†; Garden Candy Color Set
RECIPE:	Buttercream Icing, p. 101
ALSO:	Pumpkin Eye, Nose, Mouth Patterns, p. 116; Smiling Pumpkin Standard and Mini Baking Cups; Cake Boards; Parchment Triangles; spearmint jelly leaves, scissors, waxed paper

See "Wilton Products", p. 118-127 for most Wilton items used in this project.

In advance: Make candy facial features. Trace patterns on parchment paper; tape to cake board and cover with waxed paper. Tint a portion of melted yellow candy black using candy color. Pipe in noses, mouths and eyes; refrigerate until firm. Pipe in pupils; refrigerate until firm.

Ice cupcakes smooth; form section lines with edge of spatula. Position facial features. Cut strips from spearmint leaves; attach with icing for stem.

† Brand confectionery coating.

Clawing His > Way Back

PAN:	Standard Muffin
TIPS:	3, 233
COLORS:*	Leaf Green, Lemon Yellow, Black
RECIPE:	Buttercream Icing, p. 101
ALSO:	Smiling Pumpkin Standard Baking Cups; Light Cocoa Candy Melts®†; Hallow Pumpkin Mix Sprinkle Decorations; Rolling Pin; fruit jelly discs, large chocolate nougat candies, granulated sugar, scissors, paring knife, waxed paper, cornstarch

See "Wilton Products", p. 118-127 for most Wilton items used in this project.

Cover cupcake top with tip 233 pull-out grass. Position sprinkles. Insert nougat candy in center of cupcake. Roll out fruit disc on waxed paper sprinkled with sugar; cut hand shape. Pipe tip 3 bead fingernails (pat smooth with finger dipped in cornstarch). Attach hand to arm with melted candy.

* Combine Leaf Green with Lemon Yellow for green shown.

Aerial Burial

PANS: Standard Muffin; Cookie Sheet; Cooling Grid

TIPS: 1, 2, 3, 4, 6

COLORS:* Lemon Yellow, Golden Yellow, Black, Leaf Green

RECIPES: Buttercream, Royal Icings, p. 101; Roll-Out Cookie, p. 103

ALSO: Cupcakes 'N More® Standard Dessert Stand (holds 23); Spooky Ghost Standard Baking Cups; 101 Cookie Cutters Set; Halloween Mini Cutter Set; Oval Cut-Outs™; White Candy Melts®†; 4 in. Lollipop Sticks; Halloween Nonpareils Sprinkle Decorations; Petite Ghosts Icing Decorations; Rolling Pin; Meringue Powder

See "Wilton Products", p. 118-127 for most Wilton items used in this project.

In advance: Make cookies. Tint portion of cookie dough gray. Roll out dough. Cut skull and bat cookies using mini cutters. Cut moon using largest round cutter from 101 cutter set; recut to form a crescent shape. Cut gray tombstones using largest oval Cut-Out; trim level at bottom. Thin additional gray dough with water; pipe tip 6 outline trim around tombstones. Bake and cool all cookies.

Place cookies on cooling grid over drip pan; cover with thinned royal icing. Let dry. Decorate cookies with full-strength royal icing. Pipe tip 2 dot and outline facial features on skull; position orange nonpareil pupils. Print tip 2 RIP on tombstones.

Pipe tip 1 dot and string facial features on bat. Attach bat on moon with icing. Cut lollipop stick to 3 in. for moon and 2½ in. for tombstones and skulls; attach to back of cookies with melted candy, leaving 1¼ in. extended.

Ice cupcakes smooth in buttercream; sprinkle with nonpareils. Insert skulls into cupcakes. Pipe tip 4 outline and dot arms; add tip 3 outline fingers. Insert tombstone and moon cookies. Attach Petite Ghosts with icing. Position cupcakes on stand.

*Combine Lemon Yellow with Golden Yellow for yellow shown.

‹Frightful Flight

PANS: Standard Muffin; Cookie Sheet; Cooling Grid
TIPS: 1, 2, 16
COLORS:* Violet, Black, Rose, Lemon Yellow, Golden Yellow, Orange, Leaf Green
RECIPES: Buttercream, Royal Icings, p. 101; Roll-Out Cookie, p. 103
ALSO: Spooky Ghost Standard Baking Cups; 12-Pc. Halloween Mini Cutter Set; Rolling Pin; Meringue Powder
See "Wilton Products", p. 118-127 for most Wilton items used in this project.

In advance: Make cookies. Roll out cookie dough. Cut cookies using bat cutter; bake and cool. Place cookies on cooling grid over drip pan; cover with thinned royal icing. Let dry. Decorate cookies with full-strength royal icing. Pipe tip 1 dot eyes, pupils and nose, outline mouth. Add tip 2 pull-out ears; let dry.

Ice cupcakes smooth in buttercream. Pipe tip 16 star moon. Print tip 2 "EEK"; add tip 1 outline drips beneath letters. Position bat cookie.

*Combine Violet with Rose for violet shown. Combine Lemon Yellow with Golden Yellow for yellow shown.

Witch Wear ›

PANS: Cookie Sheet; Cooling Grid
TIPS: 3, 4, 47, 127D
COLORS:* Black, Violet, Rose, Orange, Lemon Yellow, Leaf Green
RECIPES: Buttercream, Royal Icings, p. 101
ALSO: Halloween Silicone Baking Cups; Meringue Powder; sugar ice cream cones, cornstarch, sharp embroidery scissors
See "Wilton Products", p. 118-127 for most Wilton items used in this project.

In advance: Make hats. Using scissors, cut cone to 3½ in. by snipping in small increments along open end. Cover cone with tip 4 zigzags in royal icing (smooth with finger dipped in cornstarch). For a smooth finish, cover cones again with thinned royal icing; let dry. Using full-strength royal icing, pipe tip 47 (smooth side up) double-width outline hat band; smooth with spatula. Pipe tip 3 outline buckle and tip 4 dots (pat smooth with finger dipped in cornstarch).

Bake and cool cupcakes in silicone cups supported by cookie sheet; ice smooth in buttercream. Pipe tip 127D ruffle brim, letting ¼ in. of ruffle extend over edge. Position hats.

*Combine Violet with Rose for violet shown.

‹ Don't Bat an Eye!

PANS: Standard Muffin; Cookie Sheet; Cooling Grid

TIPS: 3, 5

COLORS:* Leaf Green, Lemon Yellow, Black

RECIPES: Buttercream, Chocolate Buttercream Icings, p. 101; Chocolate Roll-Out Cookie, p. 103

ALSO: Spooky Ghost Standard Baking Cups; Leaves and Acorns Nesting Metal Cutter Set; Rolling Pin; chocolate chips, cornstarch

See "Wilton Products", p. 118-127 for most Wilton items used in this project.

Roll out cookie dough; cut wing cookies using smallest oak leaf cutter. Bake and cool. Ice cupcakes smooth in chocolate. Pipe tip 5 ball eyes and dot pupils (flatten and smooth with finger dipped in cornstarch). Pipe tip 3 outline mouth and pull-out fangs. Pipe tip 5 ball nose (flatten and smooth with finger). Insert wings. Attach chocolate chip ears with dots of icing.

*Combine Leaf Green with Lemon Yellow for green shown.

The Vampire Retires ›

PANS: Mini Loaf; Non-Stick Cookie Sheet

TIPS: 2, 3, 4, 6, 12

COLORS:* Leaf Green, Lemon Yellow, Black, Red-Red, Christmas Red

CANDY:* Candy Melts®† in White, Light Cocoa; Primary, Garden Candy Color Sets; Candy Melting Plate; 4 in. Lollipop Sticks

RECIPES: Buttercream, Chocolate Buttercream Icings, p. 101

ALSO: White Petite Loaf Baking Cups; Parchment Triangles; waxed paper

See "Wilton Products", p. 118-127 for most Wilton items used in this project.

In advance: Make candy faces (p. 112) using melted candy tinted green and black. Pipe hair, facial features and ears using melted candy in cut parchment bag; let set. Cut lollipop stick to 2½ in.; attach face with melted candy. **Also:** Make open lid. Pipe a 2 x 1⅝ in. cocoa candy rectangle, ⅛ in. thick, on non-stick pan; refrigerate until firm.

For closed lid, pipe tip 12 bands on mini loaf cake, overpiping as needed; smooth and shape in a curve with spatula. Pipe tip 4 zigzag sheet; smooth with spatula; add tip 4 outline pillow. Build up tip 12 body, 1¼ in. long. Pipe tip 3 outline collar. Add tip 12 outline resting arm with tip 2 dot hand and outline fingers. Pipe tip 6 outline around edge of cake. Insert head in cake. Pipe tip 4 bead and dot bow tie. Make upright arm using bag fitted with tip 12; insert a lollipop stick cut to 2½ in., extending 1 in. from bag. Squeeze and pull out stick. Insert upright arm in cake. Ice inside of open lid smooth; position on cake against arm. Pipe tip 2 dot hand and outline fingers.

*Combine green with yellow colors for green candy and icing shades shown. Combine Red-Red with Christmas Red for red shown. † Brand confectionery coating.

‹Monster Marriage

PAN:	Mini Loaf
TIPS:	1, 2, 3, 4, 6, 8, 12
COLORS:*	Black, Leaf Green, Lemon Yellow, Red-Red, Christmas Red
RECIPE:	Buttercream Icing, p. 101
ALSO:	Gold Foil Petite Loaf Cups; black spice drops, cornstarch

See "Wilton Products", p. 118-127 for most Wilton items used in this project.

Ice cakes smooth. For him, outline and pipe in hair with tip 4. Pipe tip 12 outline eyebrow and bead nose. Pipe tip 8 ball nostrils. Pipe in tip 3 whites of eyes and pupils (pat smooth with finger dipped in cornstarch). Pipe tip 4 zigzag mouth and tip 2 outline scar. For her, pipe tip 6 zigzag hair, bead nose and dot nostrils. Pipe in tip 8 ball eyes and dot pupils; add tip 3 outline eyelids. Pipe tip 1 outline eyelashes. Pipe tip 6 bead heart lips. Add tip 2 zigzag mouth and tip 4 dot cheeks. For bolts on both cakes, cut spice drops in half; attach to sides with icing.

*Combine Leaf Green with Lemon Yellow for green shown. Combine Red-Red with Christmas Red for red shown.

Cupcake Crawler ›

PANS:	Standard Muffin; Cookie Sheet; Cooling Grid
TIPS:	2, 3, 16
COLORS:*	Leaf Green, Lemon Yellow, Black
RECIPES:	Buttercream Icing, p. 101; Roll-Out Cookie, p. 103
ALSO:	Spider Leg Pattern, p. 114; Spooky Ghost Standard Baking Cups, Round Cut-Outs™; Rolling Pin; toothpick, cornstarch, paring knife

See "Wilton Products", p. 118-127 for most Wilton items used in this project.

In advance: Tint cookie dough green. Roll out and cut head using medium Cut-Out. Roll dough into ½ in. diameter rope. Cut into 4 in. lengths and position on cookie sheet to form legs following pattern shape (reverse pattern for left legs). Make 8 legs for each cupcake. Bake and cool.

On cupcake top, pipe tip 16 pull-out star body. On head, pipe tip 3 ball eyes, tip 2 dot pupils and nose. Outline mouth with tip 2. Position head on front of cupcake; insert legs.

*Combine Leaf Green with Lemon Yellow for green shown.

Delicious Devils

PANS: Mini Muffin; Cookie Sheet; Cooling Grid
TIPS: 1, 5
COLORS:* Red-Red, Christmas Red, Black
RECIPE: Buttercream Icing, p. 101
ALSO: Halloween Silicone Baking Cups; White Mini Baking Cups; Rolling Pin; waxed paper, granulated sugar, scissors, spice drops, large gum drops, jelly fruit slices, hollow-center round candy

See "Wilton Products", p. 118-127 for most Wilton items used in this project.

Bake and cool cupcakes in mini pan and silicone cups supported by cookie sheet. Ice smooth. For face cupcakes, roll out fruit slices, spice drops or gum drops on waxed paper sprinkled with sugar; cut eye, mouth and pupil shapes. Attach candy with icing. For eyeball cupcakes, position hollow-center candy. Pipe tip 5 dot pupil at center. Pipe tip 1 vein lines on eyes.

*Combine Red-Red with Christmas Red for red shown.

‹ Tom Turkey Time!

PAN: Standard Muffin

TIPS: 3, 8, 352

COLORS:* Red-Red, Orange, Brown, Black, Lemon Yellow, Golden Yellow

RECIPE: Buttercream Icing, p. 101

ALSO: Cake Board or serving plate; Fanci-Foil Wrap

See "Wilton Products", p. 118-127 for most Wilton items used in this project.

Bake and cool cupcakes without baking cups. Cut vertically in half; position cut side down (narrow end will be the front) on foil-covered board or serving plate. Starting on narrow end of cupcake, pipe 3 rows of tip 352 pull-out feathers in yellow. Pipe tip 8 upright shell neck and ball head; add tip 3 pull-out beak, string waddle and dot eyes. Pipe 3 rows of tip 352 pull-out feathers each in orange and red to cover cupcake.

✳ Combine Lemon Yellow with Golden Yellow for yellow shown.

Perfect Pies ›

PAN: Jumbo Muffin

TIPS: 5, 47, 103

COLOR: Ivory

RECIPE: Buttercream Icing, p. 101

ALSO: White Jumbo Baking Cups; cherry pie filling

See "Wilton Products", p. 118-127 for most Wilton items used in this project.

Fill cups 1/3 high with batter to create cakes that bake to 3/4 of baking cup height; bake and cool. Ice cupcakes smooth; pipe a tip 5 line on inside edge of baking cup. Cut cherries in half and top cupcakes with 1 tablespoon filling; level with spoon. Pipe tip 47 smooth side up lattice. Pipe tip 103 ruffle on edge of cupcake.

‹Rake in the Treats

PAN: Standard Muffin
COLORS:* Ivory, Orange, Brown, Golden Yellow
FONDANT: White Ready-To-Use Rolled Fondant; Rolling Pin; Roll & Cut Mat
RECIPE: Buttercream Icing, p. 101
ALSO: Harvest Mini Metal Cutter Set; White Standard Baking Cups; Fine Tip Primary Colors FoodWriter™ Edible Color Markers; Flower Former Set; Gum-Tex™; cornstarch

See "Wilton Products", p. 118-127 for most Wilton items used in this project.

In advance: Make leaves. Mix 1 teaspoon Gum-Tex with 12 oz. fondant (for about 40 leaves); tint yellow. Roll out 1/8 in. thick. Cut oak and maple leaves using cutters from set. Let dry on small flower formers dusted with cornstarch; use both sides of flower formers to vary shape. Draw vein lines with FoodWriters.

Ice cupcakes smooth. Position leaves.

＊Combine Ivory, Orange and Brown icing colors for burnt orange shown.

Huge Harvest ›

PANS: Standard Muffin; Cookie Sheet; Cooling Grid
TIP: 2
COLORS: Orange, Kelly Green, Ivory
RECIPES: Buttercream, Color Flow Icings, p. 101; Roll-Out Cookie, p. 103
ALSO: Autumn Leaves Standard Baking Cups; Leaves Mix Sprinkle Decorations; Nesting Pumpkins Cutter Set; Color Flow Mix; Rolling Pin; Parchment Triangles

See "Wilton Products", p. 118-127 for most Wilton items used in this project.

One day in advance: Make cookies. Roll out dough; cut cookies with 2¼ in. pumpkin cutter. Bake and cool. Pipe tip 2 zigzag stem in buttercream. Outline pumpkin with tip 2 and full-strength color flow; flow in with thinned color flow in cut parchment bag. Let dry.

Ice cupcakes smooth. Sprinkle with leaves mix. Insert cookie.

Big Events, Big Impact!

For their size, no dessert packs a bigger punch than cupcakes!
While a full-sized cake is magnificent at the center of your celebration,
with cupcakes, you can create a complete
decorating statement on everyone's plate.

The treats shown here are a great example—cupcakes that greet
everyone at the shower with the pitter patter of little fondant feet or
a cute cookie baby. Elsewhere, cupcakes are transformed into baby
cradles, graduation caps and fruit baskets, simply by adding fondant
or cookie toppers to the basic cake. They bring the fun right to
the table—it's no wonder cupcakes are showing up
at all kinds of special events!

Shown: *Baby Steps & Noisy Newborns*; instructions, p. 95.

Baby's Bassinette

PANS: Standard Muffin, Mini Egg, Non-Stick Cookie Sheet, Cooling Grid

TIPS: 1, 101

RECIPE: Buttercream Icing, p. 101

ALSO: Bow Pattern, p. 116; Round Metal Cookie Cutter; Round Cut-Outs™; White Candy Melts®†; 4 in. Lollipop Sticks; Parchment Triangles; Cake Release; Pastry Brush; paring knife, waxed paper

See "Wilton Products", p. 118-127 for most Wilton items used in this project.

Reserve 8 Candy Melts wafers per bassinette for wheels. Make candy shell hood (p. 113). With knife, cut off lower ⅓ of shell; smooth cut edge with finger. For top and bottom of platform, position round cutter and large Cut-Out on cookie sheet; fill each ¼ in. deep with melted candy. Refrigerate until firm; unmold. Cover bow pattern with waxed paper; outline and pipe in with melted candy in cut parchment bag. Refrigerate until firm.

Brush muffin pan with Cake Release; bake and cool cupcakes without baking cups. Turn cupcakes narrow end up and cover with melted candy (p. 106). Let set. Turn over; ice top smooth in buttercream. Attach hood with icing. Using knife, dig 4 holes in both top and bottom platform candies for legs; use lollipop sticks to line up holes. Cut 4 sticks to 2½ in.; dip ends in melted candy and insert in holes. Let set. Attach carriage to top platform with melted candy. Pipe tip 101 ruffle on edge of cupcake and hood. Add tip 1 vine and dot flowers on cupcake side. Attach wheels to sticks with candy. Attach bow to hood with icing.

† Brand confectionery coating.

< Your New Set of Wheels!

PANS: Jumbo Muffin
TIPS: 5, 101
COLORS:* Lemon Yellow, Violet, Rose
FONDANT: White Ready-To-Use Rolled Fondant; 9 in. Rolling Pin; Roll & Cut Mat; Heart Cut-Outs™
RECIPE: Buttercream Icing, p. 101
ALSO: White Jumbo Baking Cups; 4 in. Lollipop Sticks; toothpick

See "Wilton Products", p. 118-127 for most Wilton items used in this project.

Ice cupcakes smooth in white. With toothpick, mark iced top horizontally in half, then mark top portion vertically in half. Using tip 5, outline and pipe in bottom half of buggy; smooth with spatula. Pipe tip 5 lines for hood; add tip 101 ruffle. Tint portions of fondant violet and rose. For wheels, roll two ³⁄₄ in. balls; flatten and indent center with end of rolling pin. Poke holes using lollipop stick. Shape a 1¹⁄₂ in. long x ¹⁄₈ in. wide log for handle; attach with dots of icing. Roll out rose fondant ¹⁄₈ in. thick; cut heart using smallest Cut-Out. Position on cupcake.

*** Combine Violet with Rose for violet shown.

Cradled Cuties >

PANS: Mini Egg; Cookie Sheet
TIPS: 2, 6
COLORS: Kelly Green, Copper (skin tone), Lemon Yellow
FONDANT: White Ready-To-Use Rolled Fondant; Cutter/Embosser; Rolling Pin; Roll & Cut Mat; Brush Set
RECIPE: Buttercream Icing, p. 101
ALSO: Pastel Silicone Baking Cups; Fine Tip Primary Colors FoodWriter™ Edible Color Markers; Gum-Tex™; Cake Board; craft knife, cornstarch

See "Wilton Products", p. 118-127 for most Wilton items used in this project.

Several days in advance: Make heads, hands and cradle hoods. Add 1 teaspoon Gum-Tex to 12 oz. rolled fondant (for approximately 6 cupcakes). Tint a 2 in. ball copper; tint equal portions of remainder green and yellow. For hood, dust inside of egg pan cavities with cornstarch. Roll out green and yellow fondant ¹⁄₈ in. thick; cut to fit inside cavities. Trim 1¹⁄₂ in. off narrow end. Let dry in pan cavities. For heads, roll ³⁄₄ in. balls of copper fondant; for hands roll ¹⁄₄ in. balls. Flatten hands and score finger lines with knife. Let dry on cornstarch-dusted board.

Bake and cool cupcakes in silicone cups supported by cookie sheet. Ice smooth. Roll out white fondant ¹⁄₈ in. thick. Cut a semi-circle to cover top curve of cupcake for bedsheet; position. For blanket, cut a 3 x 2¹⁄₂ in. fondant rectangle; score quilt lines in ³⁄₈ in. squares with smooth-edge wheel of Cutter/Embosser. For body, pipe a tip 6 mound of icing to give dimension under blanket. Fold over ¹⁄₂ in. of blanket and position on cupcake. Draw facial features with black FoodWriter. Roll a tiny ball for nose; attach with damp brush. Attach head and hands with icing. Attach hood with icing. Pipe tip 2 beads on edge, tip 2 dots where quilt squares meet.

‹ A Bib Over All

PAN:	Standard Muffin
TIPS:	2, 3, 7
COLORS:	Royal Blue, Rose, Lemon Yellow
FONDANT:	Pastel Colors Fondant Multi Pack; Rolling Pin; Roll & Cut Mat; Flower Cut-Outs™
RECIPE:	Buttercream Icing, p. 101
ALSO:	Assorted Pastel Standard Baking Cups; Angled Spatula; Cake Board; ¼ in. white satin ribbon (6 in. per bow), cornstarch

See "Wilton Products", p. 118-127 for most Wilton items used in this project.

In advance: Make flowers. Roll out blue and pink fondant ⅛ in. thick. Cut flowers with smallest Cut-Out; let dry on cornstarch-dusted board.

Ice cupcakes smooth in yellow. Pipe white bib area with tip 7 zigzags (smooth with finger dipped in cornstarch); leave a 1¼ x 1½ in. area for opening. Insert flowers on edge of cupcake. Pipe tip 3 bead border on neckline. Print tip 2 message. Tie ribbon into bow; attach with dots of icing.

Little Peepers ›

PAN:	Cookie Sheet
TIP:	2
COLORS:	Royal Blue, Lemon Yellow, Rose, Copper (skin tone), Brown
FONDANT:	White Ready-To-Use Rolled Fondant; Rolling Pin; Roll & Cut Mat; Cutter/Embosser; Square Cut-Outs™; Brush Set
RECIPE:	Buttercream Icing, p. 101
ALSO:	Pastel Silicone Baking Cups; Fine Tip Primary Colors FoodWriter™ Edible Color Markers; ruler, paring knife

See "Wilton Products", p. 118-127 for most Wilton items used in this project.

In advance: Make head, hands and body. For head and hands, tint a 1½ in. ball of fondant copper or light brown. Roll a 1 in. ball head and a ⅛ in. ball nose; attach nose with damp brush. Draw mouth and eyes with black FoodWriter. Roll ⅜ in. ball hands; score finger lines with knife. Attach hands to head with damp brush. For body, shape a 1¼ x ¾ in. oval of white fondant; indent at center and attach to back of head with damp brush.

Bake and cool cupcakes in silicone cups supported by cookie sheet. Ice smooth. Position baby pieces. To make 2 blankets, tint 1½ in. balls each in light yellow, light blue and light rose; reserve remaining white fondant. Roll out all fondant 1/16 in. thick. Cut a 3½ x 3 in. base piece in white. Using smallest Cut-Out, cut 5 squares in each color (including white) for each blanket. Attach squares to base with damp brush, alternating colors with white. Smooth gaps with fingers. Position blanket. Pipe tip 2 pull-out fringe. For pacifier, roll a ¼ in. oval in blue or pink and a 1/16 in. ball in white for center. Attach with damp brush.

Party Pacifiers >

PANS: 8 x 2 in. Square; Non-Stick Cookie Sheet; Cooling Grid
CANDY: White Candy Melts®†; Primary Candy Color Set
ALSO: 101 Cookie Cutters Set; Round Cut-Outs™; paring knife
See "Wilton Products", p. 118-127 for most Wilton items used in this project.

Bake and cool 1-layer square cake (use firm-textured batter such as pound cake); cut into two 1 in. high layers. Using medium round cookie cutter, cut out cake circles. Using medium Cut-Out, imprint a center circle; cut out with knife. Cut a gingerbread boy shape using small cookie cutter from set; use head and neck area to make nipple and remove lower body areas. Place cakes on cooling grid over cookie sheet. Tint portions of white candy blue, yellow and pink using candy colors. Cover cakes with melted candy; let dry. Turn cakes over and coat bottom with candy. For base and center of pacifier, place large round cookie cutter and medium Cut-Out on cookie sheet; fill large cutter ¼ in. high with white and medium Cut-Out ⅛ in. high with pink melted candy; refrigerate until firm. Attach candy to cakes with melted candy.

† Brand confectionery coating.

^ Baby Shakes It Up

PANS: Standard Muffin
TIPS: 3, 18
COLOR: Lemon Yellow
FONDANT: Pastel Colors Fondant Multi Pack; Flower Cut-Outs™; Rolling Pin; Roll & Cut Mat
RECIPE: Buttercream Icing, p. 101
ALSO: White Standard Baking Cups; 4 in. Lollipop Sticks; Cake Board; ¼ in. satin ribbon (14 in. per bow), scissors, cornstarch
See "Wilton Products", p. 118-127 for most Wilton items used in this project.

In advance: Make flowers. Roll out fondant ⅛ in. thick; cut flowers using smallest Cut-Out. Let dry on cornstarch-dusted board.

Ice cupcakes smooth. Pipe tip 18 zigzag garland; position flowers. Add tip 3 dot flower centers. Tie ribbon in a bow around lollipop stick; trim as needed. Attach flower to end of stick with dots of icing. Insert stick in cupcake.

^ Her First Accessory

PAN: Cookie Sheet
COLOR: Rose
FONDANT: White Ready-To-Use Rolled Fondant; Rolling Pin; Roll & Cut Mat
RECIPE: Buttercream Icing, p. 101
ALSO: Pin Head Pattern, p. 116; Pastel Silicone Baking Cups; 4 in. Lollipop Sticks; Gum-Tex™; Cake Board; waxed paper, paring knife, cornstarch, toothpick
See "Wilton Products", p. 118-127 for most Wilton items used in this project.

Two days in advance: Make pin. Add ½ teaspoon Gum-Tex to 8 oz. fondant; tint rose. Roll out ⅛ in. thick. Trace pin head pattern with toothpick; cut out with knife. Shape a 1 in. ball of fondant into an 8 in. rope, ¼ in. thick; twist and bend to form bottom of pin. Cut a lollipop stick into 2 in. lengths; insert ½ in. deep into each end of log. Let dry 48 hours on waxed paper-covered board dusted with cornstarch.

Bake and cool cupcakes in silicone cups supported by cookie sheet. Ice smooth. Insert bottom of pin; position pin head.

^ Scholastic Stars

PANS: Standard Muffin; Cookie Sheet; Cooling Grid

TIP: 5

COLORS:* Lemon Yellow, Golden Yellow, Red-Red, Christmas Red

RECIPES: Buttercream Icing, p. 101; Roll-Out Cookie, p. 103

ALSO: Smiley Grad Standard Baking Cups; Star Cut-Outs™; Stars Jumbo Sprinkle Decorations; Yellow Colored Sugar; Rolling Pin

See "Wilton Products", p. 118-127 for most Wilton items used in this project.

Tint cookie dough yellow. Roll out and cut cookies using largest Cut-Out. Sprinkle with sugar; bake and cool. Pipe tip 5 numbers.

Ice cupcakes smooth. Insert cookies, adding icing to support as needed. Attach star sprinkles to cookie with icing; position additional sprinkles on cupcake.

***Combine Lemon Yellow with Golden Yellow for yellow shown. Combine Red-Red with Christmas Red for red shown.**

^ Senior Smiles

PANS: Standard Muffin; Cooling Grid

CANDY: White Candy Melts®†; Smiley Face Candy Mold; Primary, Garden Candy Color Sets; 4 in. Lollipop Sticks

RECIPE: Buttercream Icing, p. 101

ALSO: Smiley Grad Standard Baking Cups; Jumbo Nonpareils Sprinkle Decorations; Parchment Triangles; large hollow-center hard candy disks, sturdy cardboard, white paper, waxed paper

See "Wilton Products", p. 118-127 for most Wilton items used in this project.

Tint portions of Candy Melts yellow, blue and black using candy colors. Mold face lollipops in yellow; refrigerate until firm and unmold. Using melted black candy in cut parchment bag, pipe dot eyes and string mouth; refrigerate until firm. For mortarboards, make a 1½ in. square pattern on white paper; tape to cardboard and cover with waxed paper. Using melted blue candy in cut parchment bag, pipe in pattern. Tap to level; refrigerate until firm. Position hard candies on cooling grid over pan; cover with melted blue candy. Refrigerate until firm. Attach hard candies to mortarboards and mortarboards to faces with melted candy; let set. Ice cupcakes smooth; sprinkle with nonpareils. Trim lollipop sticks to 2 in.; insert faces in cupcakes.

† Brand confectionery coating.

< Looking Smart

PAN: Standard Muffin

TIPS: 2, 3

COLORS:* Black, Brown, Copper (skin tone), Red-Red, Christmas Red

FONDANT: White Ready-To-Use Rolled Fondant; Primary Colors Fondant Multi Pack; Square Cut-Outs™; Rolling Pin; Roll & Cut Mat; Brush Set

RECIPE: Buttercream Icing, p. 101

ALSO: Graduation Standard Baking Cups; Gum-Tex™; Cake Board; cornstarch

See "Wilton Products", p. 118-127 for most Wilton items used in this project.

Several days in advance: Make mortarboards. Mix a 1½ in. ball of white fondant with ½ pack of blue fondant. Add ½ teaspoon Gum-Tex each to 3 in. balls of blue and white fondant. Roll out 1⁄16 in. thick. Cut squares using largest Cut-Out. Let dry on cornstarch-dusted boards.

Ice cupcakes smooth. Pipe tip 3 dot eyes, pupils, nose and cheeks (flatten and smooth with finger dipped in cornstarch). Outline and pipe in tip 3 mouth. Pipe tip 2 bead tongue. Add tip 3 swirl hair. Attach mortarboard with icing. For tassel, roll out yellow fondant 1⁄16 in. thick. Cut a 1½ x 1 in. rectangle; cut slits ½ in. deep on one long side. Roll up to form tassel; shape a rounded top just above fringe. For cord, cut a strip ¼ x 2 in. long; press tassel on cord. Attach to mortarboard with damp brush. Roll a ¼ in. fondant ball for button and attach to top with damp brush.

***Combine Red-Red with Christmas Red for red shown.**

‹ Goody For the Grad!

PANS:	Standard Muffin; Cookie Sheet; Cooling Grid
TIP:	6
COLOR:	Royal Blue
RECIPES:	Buttercream Icing, p. 101; Roll-Out Cookie, p. 103
ALSO:	Spatula; Cake Release; Pastry Brush; Rolling Pin, paring knife, yellow taffy, scissors, cornstarch, ruler

See "Wilton Products", p. 118-127 for most Wilton items used in this project.

Tint cookie dough blue; roll out and cut 3½ in. square cookies using ruler and paring knife. Bake and cool.

Brush pan cavities with Cake Release. Bake and cool cupcakes without baking cups; level tops. Turn cupcakes narrow end up. Ice cupcakes and cookies smooth; position cookie on cupcake. Roll out taffy and cut a 2½ x ¼ in. wide strip for cord; cut a 1 in. long strip for tassel. Cut slits in tassel and press together with cord. Cut a ½ in. long strip for knot and wrap around. Attach tassel to cookie with icing. Pipe tip 6 ball button (flatten and smooth with finger dipped in cornstarch).

Memories Locked In ›

PAN:	Mini Loaf
TIPS:	3, 5
COLORS: *	Sky Blue, Orange, Lemon Yellow, Black, Leaf Green
RECIPE:	Buttercream Icing, p. 101
ALSO:	Stars Jumbo Sprinkle Decorations; Cake Release; Pastry Brush; Graduation Icing Decorations

See "Wilton Products", p. 118-127 for most Wilton items used in this project.

Brush pan cavities with Cake Release. Bake and cool cakes without cups; ice smooth. Pipe tip 5 lines for vents. Pipe tip 3 balls and outline for lock. Pipe tip 5 outline door handle. Position icing decorations and sprinkles.

＊Combine Leaf Green with Lemon Yellow for green shown.

<Berry Refreshing

PAN: Cookie Sheet

TIP: 2

COLOR: Lemon Yellow

ALSO: Heart Silicone Baking Cups; Vanilla Whipped Icing Mix; Parchment Triangles; strawberry flavor gelatin, jelly spearmint leaves, vegetable oil pan spray, paring knife

See "Wilton Products", p. 118-127 for most Wilton items used in this project.

Prepare gelatin following package directions; prepare baking cups with pan spray. Pour dissolved gelatin into baking cups supported by cookie sheet; refrigerate until firm. Cut spearmint leaves horizontally in thirds; cut each piece vertically in thirds. Insert center third in gelatin for stem; insert side thirds flat side down for leaves. Tint whipped icing yellow; pipe tip 2 bead seeds.

Fruit Basket >

PAN: Cookie Sheet

COLORS: Rose, Sky Blue

RECIPES: Buttercream Icing, p. 101

ALSO: Pastel or Square Silicone Baking Cups; White Ready-To-Use Rolled Fondant; Gum-Tex™; Cake Boards; fresh blueberries, raspberries, mint leaves, waxed paper, cornstarch

See "Wilton Products", p. 118-127 for most Wilton items used in this project.

Two days in advance: Make fondant rope basket handle (p. 113). Add 1 teaspoon Gum-Tex to 8 oz. fondant; tint portions rose and blue to match baking cups. Roll two ¼ in. diameter ropes; twist together to make handle. Position in an arched shape, 2½ in. high and 2 in. apart at bottom on waxed paper-covered board dusted with cornstarch; let dry.

Fill silicone cups half-full so that cupcakes bake ¼ in. below edge of cup. Bake and cool, supporting cups with cookie sheet. Ice smooth; insert handle. Position berries and mint leaves.

Visit the Fruit Stand!

PAN: Mini Muffin

TIP: 22

RECIPE: Buttercream Icing, p. 101

ALSO: Cupcakes 'N More® Mini Dessert Stand; White Mini Baking Cups; fresh blueberries, raspberries, mint leaves

See "Wilton Products", p. 118-127 for most Wilton items used in this project.

Cover cupcake tops with tip 22 swirl. On half of the cupcakes, position a raspberry; on remaining, position 3 blueberries. Add mint leaf on each. Position cupcakes on stand.

<Lemon Burst

PANS: Jumbo Muffin; Cookie Sheet; Cooling Grid
RECIPE: Lemon Cupcakes, p. 100
ALSO: White Ready-To-Use Decorator Icing; Cake Release; Parchment Triangles; fresh raspberries and lemons, lemon stripper

See "Wilton Products", p. 118-127 for most Wilton items used in this project.

Brush pan cavities with Cake Release. Bake and cool cakes without baking cups. Level top of cupcake and turn over on cooling grid set over cookie sheet. Heat icing following package directions; cover cupcake using heated icing in cut parchment bag. Let set. Position fresh raspberries and lemon strips.

Coffee and Dessert >

PANS: Standard Muffin; Non-Stick Cookie Sheet; Cooling Grid
TIP: 1M (2110)
RECIPES: Mocha Buttercream, p. 101; Mocha Cupcakes, p. 99
ALSO: Steam Curls, Cup Handle Patterns, p. 116; Round Comfort Grip™ Cutter; Parchment Triangles; Candy Melts®† in White, Light Cocoa; Cake Board; Cake Release; Pastry Brush; cocoa powder, waxed paper

See "Wilton Products", p. 118-127 for most Wilton items used in this project.

In advance: Make candy base, steam curls and handle. For base, position cutter on cookie sheet and fill 1/8 in. high with melted white candy; refrigerate until firm. Tape steam curls and handle patterns to cake board; cover with waxed paper. Outline patterns with melted candy in cut parchment bag; refrigerate until firm. Turn candy over and overpipe; refrigerate until firm.

Brush pan cavities with Cake Release. Bake and cool cupcakes without baking cups. Turn upside down and position on cooling grid over cookie sheet. Cover with melted white candy; let set. Turn over cupcakes; position on base and cover top with tip 1M swirl in buttercream. Attach handle with melted candy; pipe swirl trim with melted candy in cut parchment bag. Dust top with cocoa powder. Insert steam curls.

‹ Ganache Grandeur

PANS:	Tasty-Fill™ Mini Cake; Mini Loaf; Cookie Sheet; Cooling Grid
TIP:	32
RECIPES:	Chocolate Ganache, Whipped Ganache, p. 102; German Chocolate Cupcakes, p. 96; Easy Cream Filling, p. 102
ALSO:	Chocolate Swirls Pattern, p. 117; Dark Cocoa Candy Melts®†; Parchment Triangles; Cake Release; Pastry Brush; Cake Boards; 4 in. Lollipop Sticks; fresh raspberries, waxed paper, cheese plane or vegetable peeler, vegetable shortening

See "Wilton Products", p. 118-127 for most Wilton items used in this project.

In advance: Make candy swirls. Tape pattern to board; cover with waxed paper. Outline pattern with melted candy; refrigerate until firm. Turn candy over and repeat; refrigerate until firm.
Also: Make chocolate curls. Melt 1 package of Candy Melts and add 2 tablespoons of shortening. Fill 2 mini loaf cavities with melted candy; refrigerate until firm; unmold. Bring to room temperature. Shave candy plaques with cheese plane or peeler to make curls; set aside.

Brush pan cavities with Cake Release. Bake and cool cakes; fill with filling and stack. Place on cooling grid over cookie sheet. Pour chocolate ganache over cakes, covering completely. Let set. Transfer to serving plate. Using lollipop stick, make hole in cake top; insert chocolate swirls. Pipe tip 32 rosette with whipped ganache. Garnish with raspberries and chocolate curls.

† Brand confectionery coating.

Chocolate Fountain ›

PAN:	Jumbo; Mini Muffin
TIP:	1M (2110)
RECIPE:	Chocolate Mousse, p. 103
ALSO:	Chocolate Fountain Pattern, p. 116; White Jumbo, Mini Baking Cups; Light Cocoa Candy Melts®†; Cake Board; Decorator Brush Set; Parchment Triangles; waxed paper

See "Wilton Products", p. 118-127 for most Wilton items used in this project.

In advance: Make candy bases. Place mini cups in mini pan cavities and fill with melted candy; refrigerate until firm.
Also: Make candy shells. Place jumbo cups in jumbo pan cavities. Brush bottom and inside cups with melted candy to form a shell 1½ in. high; refrigerate until firm. Carefully peel off baking cups. Attach shell to base with melted candy; let set.
Also: Make 4 candy fountain pieces for each cupcake. Tape pattern to board; cover with waxed paper. Outline pattern with melted candy in cut parchment bag; refrigerate until firm. Turn candy over and repeat; refrigerate until firm.

Pipe mousse into candy shells using tip 1M. Insert candy swirls at various depths to create fountain shape.

To Have & To Hold

How did cupcakes crash the wedding? More couples than ever before are realizing the elegance and fun cupcakes can bring to the reception! Guests can't help but smile when they see these favorite treats from childhood at such a grown-up event.

All the reasons you need to invite cupcakes to the wedding, shower or anniversary are on the following pages. When cupcakes can look so sophisticated, with designs featuring tuxedos and bridal gowns, flowers or bows, they can carry your wedding theme as well as any tiered cake. Many of the same bridal motifs you would see on the main cake are here, including wedding bells, diamond rings, swans and champagne flutes. And as you can see at right, when displayed on a beautiful stand, cupcakes can also create as great an impact as a full-sized traditional wedding cake.

Shown: *Group Wedding*; instructions, p. 95.

< Two True

PANS: Jumbo Muffin; Cookie Sheet; Cooling Grid
TIPS: 1, 2, 5, 101, 352
COLORS:* Violet, Rose, Moss Green
RECIPES: Buttercream, Royal Icings, p. 101; Roll-Out Cookie, p. 103; Color Flow Icing, p. 101
ALSO: White Jumbo Baking Cups; 4 in. Lollipop Sticks; Valentine Metal Cutter Collection; Flower Nail No. 7; Color Flow Mix; Meringue Powder; Rolling Pin; Parchment Triangles; Spatula; waxed paper squares

See "Wilton Products", p. 118-127 for most Wilton items used in this project.

In advance: Make roses (p. 109). For each cupcake, make 6 tip 101 roses with tip 5 bases using royal icing. Make extras to allow for breakage and let dry. **Also:** Make cookies. Roll out dough. Cut heart cookies using crinkle cutter; bake and cool. Outline cookies with tip 2 and full-strength color flow. Pipe in using thinned color flow in cut parchment bag; let set. Pipe tip 1 name, dots and curliques in full-strength color flow. Attach cookies to sticks with full-strength color flow; let dry.

Ice cupcakes smooth in buttercream. Insert cookies. Position roses. Pipe tip 352 leaves.

✳ Combine Violet with Rose for violet shown.

The Couple's Corsage >

PAN: Cookie Sheet
TIPS: 3, 5, 101, 349
COLORS: Rose, Moss Green
RECIPES: Buttercream, Royal Icings, p. 101
ALSO: Heart Silicone Baking Cups; Meringue Powder; Disposable Decorating Bags; Flower Nail No. 7; Spatula; waxed paper squares

See "Wilton Products", p. 118-127 for most Wilton items used in this project.

In advance: Make roses (p. 109). For each cupcake, make 5 tip 101 roses with tip 5 bases using royal icing. Make extras to allow for breakage and let dry.

Bake and cool cupcakes in silicone cups supported by cookie sheet. Ice smooth in buttercream. Position roses; add tip 349 leaves. Pipe tip 3 monogram.

< Love in Lace

PAN: Standard Muffin; Cookie Sheet
RECIPES: Buttercream Icing, p. 101; German Chocolate Cupcakes, p. 96
ALSO: White Standard Baking Cups; Cupcake Pedestals; Parchment Triangles; Light Cocoa Candy Melts®†; Heart Cut-Outs™; Spatula; waxed paper, white paper

See "Wilton Products", p. 118-127 for most Wilton items used in this project.

In advance: Make candy hearts. Trace medium heart Cut-Out on paper; tape to cookie sheet. Cut waxed paper to cover pattern and tape to secure. Outline heart pattern using melted candy in parchment bag cut with tiny opening. Pipe lace-look outlines on inside of heart; edge heart with dots. Pipe a spike at bottom of each for inserting into cupcake. Refrigerate until firm.

Ice cupcakes smooth. To release heart from waxed paper, carefully slide a sheet of paper underneath and lift off. Insert in cupcake. Position cupcakes on pedestals.

† Brand confectionery coating.

Cheesecake Tiers >

PANS: Standard; Mini Muffin
ALSO: Tapered Spatula; favorite no-bake cheesecake mix, fresh raspberries, mint leaves

See "Wilton Products", p. 118-127 for most Wilton items used in this project.

Prepare cheesecake mix and graham cracker crust. Press crust onto bottom of standard and mini muffin pan cavities. Fill with cheesecake mixture; refrigerate until firm. Place in freezer for 1 hour before unmolding. To unmold, slide blade of spatula around inside edge of cavity then lift from pan. Smooth sides with spatula if needed. Position mini on standard cheesecake. Garnish with raspberry and mint leaves.

< Swimming Swans

PAN:	Standard Muffin
TIPS:	1A (2110), 3, 12, 352
COLOR:	Royal Blue
RECIPES:	Buttercream, Royal Icings, p. 101
ALSO:	Head, Wings Patterns, p. 117; Silver Foil Standard Baking Cups; Cupcake Pedestals; Fine Tip Primary Colors FoodWriter™ Edible Color Markers; Cake Boards; Meringue Powder; Spatula; waxed paper, cornstarch

See "Wilton Products", p. 118-127 for most Wilton items used in this project.

At least 2 days in advance: Make swan head and wings. Tape patterns to cake board; cover with waxed paper. Using royal icing and tip 12, pipe ball head with heavy pressure; decrease pressure as you pipe outline neck. Pipe tip 3 pull-out beak. Pipe tip 352 pull-out wings. Let dry overnight. Carefully remove head from waxed paper; turn over and overpipe back with tip 12 (pat seam to blend with finger dipped in cornstarch). Overpipe beak with tip 3. Let dry overnight. Draw dot eyes with black FoodWriter.

Ice cupcakes smooth in buttercream. Pipe tip 1A shell-motion body using heavy pressure; decrease pressure toward tail and raise tip to create a lifted tail. Insert head and wings. Pipe tip 352 pull-out tail feathers in buttercream. Position on pedestals.

A Romantic Ring >

PANS:	Standard Muffin; Cookie Sheet; Cooling Grid
TIPS:	1, 6, 12
COLOR:	Rose
RECIPES:	Buttercream, Royal Icings, p. 101; Roll-Out Cookie, p. 103
ALSO:	Bow Pattern, p. 117; Silver Foil Standard Baking Cups; Mini Romantic Metal Cutter Set; Cake Board; Rolling Pin; Meringue Powder; Spatula; waxed paper

See "Wilton Products", p. 118-127 for most Wilton items used in this project.

In advance: Make bow. Tape pattern to board; cover with waxed paper. Using royal icing and tip 6, pipe bow. Make extras to allow for breakage and let dry. **Also:** Make bells. Roll out dough. Using bell cutter, cut 2 cookies for each cupcake. Bake and cool; place on cooling grid over cookie sheet. Thin a portion of royal icing with water and pour over cookies; let dry. Position on waxed paper. Using full-strength royal icing, pipe tip 1 outline trims on bells; add tip 6 dot clappers. Let dry.

Ice cupcakes smooth in buttercream. Pipe a tip 12 mound of icing at center to support cookies; position cookies, so that tops touch. Using royal icing and tip 6, attach bow to cookies. Let dry.

‹ Gem Dandy

PANS: Standard Muffin; Cookie Sheet; Cooling Grid
TIPS: 3, 129, 224, 352
COLORS: Black, Lemon Yellow, Rose, Kelly Green
RECIPES: Buttercream, Royal Icings, p. 101; Roll-Out Cookie, p. 103
ALSO: White Standard Baking Cups; Round Cut-Outs™; Rolling Pin; 4 in. Lollipop Sticks; Meringue Powder; Cake Board; Spatula; large gumdrops, waxed paper

See "Wilton Products", p. 118-127 for most Wilton items used in this project.

In advance: Make ring cookie. Roll out dough; cut circle using largest Cut-Out. Cut center from circle using medium Cut-Out; remove center dough. Bake and cool. With royal icing, outline ring with tip 3; pipe in with thinned royal icing. Let dry. Cut 1/2 in. off lollipop stick; attach to back of cookie on one side using full-strength royal icing. Let dry. **Also:** Make flowers in royal icing. For each cookie pipe one tip 224 yellow and two tip 129 rose drop flowers; add tip 3 white dot centers. Make extras to allow for breakage and let dry.

Ice cupcakes smooth in buttercream. Insert ring cookie. Attach gumdrop to top edge of cookie using royal icing. Pipe tip 3 outline prongs in royal icing. Position drop flowers, add tip 352 leaves using buttercream icing.

Toast Them Together ›

PANS: Standard Muffin
TIP: 5
FONDANT: White Ready-To-Use Rolled Fondant; Cutter/Embosser; Rolling Pin; Roll & Cut Mat; Oval Cut-Outs™; Brush Set
RECIPES: Buttercream Icing, p. 101; Thinned Fondant Adhesive, p. 102
ALSO: Gold Foil Standard Baking Cups; White Nonpareils Sprinkle Decorations; Elegant Shimmer Dust™; 8 in. Cookie Treat Sticks; Decorator Brush Set; Cake Board; Spatula; ruler, waxed paper, cornstarch

See "Wilton Products", p. 118-127 for most Wilton items used in this project.

In advance: Make champagne flutes (1 oz. fondant will make 3 flutes). Roll out fondant 1/8 in. thick. Cut 2 ovals for each cupcake using largest Cut-Out. Cut 1/2 in. off one short side on each to be used for flute base. Let all dry on waxed paper-covered board dusted with cornstarch.

Cut cookie sticks in half. For each flute base, attach prepared 1/2 in. piece, straight side down, with adhesive, 1 1/4 in. from bottom of stick. Attach large fondant glass at top of stick, 1 in. from top of flute base. Let dry. Brush champagne portion of flute with water. Using a dry brush, paint on gold and pearl Shimmer Dust; let dry. Ice cupcakes smooth and sprinkle with nonpareils. Cover stick with tip 5 beads. Insert flutes in cupcake.

Here's To a Happy Beginning!

PANS: Mini Ball; Cookie Sheet; Cooling Grid

TIPS: 1, 2, 3, 131, 225, 349

COLORS:* Brown, Black, Kelly Green, Lemon Yellow, Copper (skin tone), Rose, Orange, Red-Red

FONDANT: White Ready-To-Use Rolled Fondant; Rolling Pin; Roll & Cut Mat; Brush Set; Cutter/Embosser

RECIPES: Buttercream, Royal Icings, p. 101; Roll-Out Cookie, p. 103

ALSO: Easel Pattern, p. 117; Tuxedo Jacket, Shirt, Lapels, Pants, Shoes, Bodice, Veil Patterns, p. 117; Gingerbread Boy Metal Cutter; 4 in. Lollipop Sticks; Piping Gel; Meringue Powder; Spatula; ruler, waxed paper, toothpick

See "Wilton Products", p. 118-127 for most Wilton items used in this project.

In advance: On waxed paper, using royal icing, make approximately 15 tip 225 drop flowers in white for each couple and 21 tip 131 drop flowers in rose for every 3 bridesmaids. Add tip 2 white dot centers. Let dry. Tint cookie dough copper. Roll out and cut cookies using boy cutter; cut bride and bridesmaid cookies at waist. Using pattern and toothpick, trace 2 easel cookies for groom; cut out. Bake and cool.

Decorate groom in royal icing. Pipe tip 2 string mouth, dot eyes, nose and cheeks. Add tip 3 string hair. Tint portion of fondant black. Roll out black and white fondant 1/8 in. thick. Using patterns, cut shirt, tuxedo jacket, lapels, pants and shoes; attach with piping gel. Shape a 3/4 x 1/4 in. log into bow tie. Cut thin strips for cuffs; attach with damp brush. Pipe tip 1 dot buttons. Using royal icing, attach easels to back of cookie; attach flower.

For bride and bridesmaids, lightly ice mini ball cakes in buttercream. Tint portion of fondant rose for bridesmaids. Cover cakes with fondant; smooth with fingers. On cookies, decorate facial features in royal icing following groom instructions; pipe tip 3 swirl hair. Roll out fondant 1/8 in. thick; cut bodice using pattern. Attach to cookie with piping gel. Pipe tip 2 bead neckline. For bride, add tip 1 dot and scroll trim on one sleeve; for bridesmaids, pipe a tip 2 outline on one sleeve. Using wide end of tip 2, cut a fondant circle. Flatten slightly and attach to other sleeve with damp brush for bouquet base. Attach flowers to base with royal icing. Pipe tip 349 leaves in royal icing. Trim lollipop stick to 3 in.; attach cookie to lollipop stick with royal icing, leaving 11/2 in. extended at bottom. Insert cookies in cakes. Cut two 1/4 x 21/4 in. fondant streamers; cut V-shape at end and attach to bouquets with damp brush. Cut a 1/4 x 2 in. strip for waistband; attach around body with damp brush. For bow, cut a 3/8 x 1 in. strip; pinch at center. Roll a small ball for knot. Attach knot and bow with damp brush. For bride, cut veil using pattern. Attach veil and flowers with royal icing.

*Combine Red-Red with Orange for red shown.

‹Bold Bows

PAN: Standard Muffin
COLORS:* Lemon Yellow, Rose, Violet, Kelly Green
FONDANT: White Ready-To-Use Rolled Fondant; Rolling Pin; Roll & Cut Mat; Cutter/Embosser; Brush Set
RECIPE: Buttercream Icing, p. 101
ALSO: White Standard Baking Cups; Gum-Tex™; Cake Board; Spatula; cornstarch

See "Wilton Products", p. 118-127 for most Wilton items used in this project.

Several days in advance: Make bows (p. 113). Add 2 teaspoons Gum-Tex to 24 oz. fondant (makes 20 to 24 bows); divide in 4ths. Tint portions yellow, rose, violet and green. Roll out fondant 1/8 in. thick. Cut ten 1/2 x 3 in. loop strips for each cupcake. Fold strips in half, brush ends with water and press together to form loops. Stand on sides on cornstarch-dusted cake board and let dry.

Ice cupcakes smooth. Position loops, securing with icing if needed.

* Combine Violet with Rose for violet shown.

Ready for Showers ›

PANS: Standard Muffin; Cookie Sheet
COLORS: Rose, Royal Blue, Lemon Yellow
FONDANT: White Ready-To-Use Rolled Fondant; Rolling Pin; Roll & Cut Mat; Round Cut-Outs™
RECIPES: Buttercream Icing, p. 101; Thinned Fondant Adhesive, p. 102
ALSO: Pastel Silicone Baking Cups; 6 in. Lollipop Sticks; Heart Drops; Spatula; Cake Board; waxed paper, cornstarch, 1/8 in. satin ribbon in pink, yellow, blue, (6 in. for each bow)

See "Wilton Products", p. 118-127 for most Wilton items used in this project.

In advance: Make umbrellas. Tint fondant rose, blue and yellow; roll out 1/8 in. thick. Cut a circle for each umbrella using largest Cut-Out; cut across circles, slightly more than halfway. Cut scalloped edge using smallest Cut-Out. Score rib lines using edge of spatula. Let dry on waxed paper-covered board dusted with cornstarch. Reserve remaining tinted fondant. Cut lollipop stick to 5 in.; attach umbella with fondant adhesive. Let set. Using reserved fondant, shape a 1/4 in. ball. Attach to umbrella top with fondant adhesive. Let set.

Bake and cool cupcakes in silicone cups supported by cookie sheet. Ice smooth; sprinkle with heart drops. Insert umbrella. Make ribbon bow; attach to stick with thinned fondant adhesive.

‹Bridal Blossoms

PANS:	Cookie Sheet
TIPS:	3, 352
COLORS:	Sky Blue, Kelly Green, Lemon Yellow
FONDANT:	White Ready-To-Use Rolled Fondant; Rolling Pin; Roll & Cut Mat; Fondant Shaping Foam
RECIPE:	Buttercream Icing, p. 101
ALSO:	Square Silicone Baking Cups; Floral Collection Flower Making Set; Confectionery Tool Set; Flower Former Set; Gum-Tex; Spatula; cornstarch, waxed paper

See "Wilton Products", p. 118-127 for most Wilton items used in this project.

Two days in advance: Make basket handle. Add 1 teaspoon Gum-Tex to 8 oz. fondant; tint blue. See Fondant Rope, (p. 113). Position in an arched shape, 2 in. high and 2 in. apart at ends on waxed paper-covered board dusted with cornstarch. Trim excess off ends and let dry. **Also:** Make Fondant Flowers, (p. 112). Cut 20 flowers for each basket using pansy cutter from Flower Making Set (make extras to allow for breakage).

Bake and cool cupcakes in silicone cups supported by cookie sheet. Ice smooth, building up to form a mound at center. Insert handle; position flowers. Pipe tip 3 dot centers in yellow. Add tip 352 leaves.

Carried When You're Married ›

PAN:	Jumbo Muffin
TIPS:	3, 352
COLORS:	Lemon Yellow, Moss Green
FONDANT:	White Ready-To-Use Rolled Fondant; Rolling Pin; Roll & Cut Mat
RECIPES:	Buttercream, Royal Icings, p. 101
ALSO:	White Jumbo Baking Cups; Floral Collection Flower Making Set; Flower Former Set; Gum-Tex™; Meringue Powder; Spatula; 1/2 in. wide white satin ribbon (12 in. for each bow), cornstarch

See "Wilton Products", p. 118-127 for most Wilton items used in this project.

In advance: Make Fondant Flowers, (p. 112). Add 1/2 teaspoon Gum-Tex to 6 oz. fondant; tint yellow. Cut 24 flowers for each cupcake using pansy cutter from Flower Making Set (make extras to allow for breakage). Add tip 3 dot flower centers in royal icing.

Ice cupcakes smooth, building up to form a mound at center. Position flowers; add tip 352 leaves. Tie a ribbon bow; attach with dots of icing.

Festive Florals

PANS: Standard Muffin

TIPS: 2D, 4, 131

COLORS: Rose, Kelly Green

RECIPES: Buttercream, Royal Icings, p. 101

ALSO: Cupcakes 'n More® Dessert Stand (holds 13); Plastic Dowel Rods; Cake Board; White Standard Baking Cups; Decorator Brush Set; Spatula; 24-gauge cloth-covered florist wire (232 pieces, 5 in. long), craft block, waxed paper, wire cutters, floral tape

See "Wilton Products", p. 118-127 for most Wilton items used in this project.

In advance: Make flowers and calyxes using royal icing (make extras of all to allow for breakage). Make 134 tip 2D (large) drop flowers and 98 tip 131 (small) drop flowers, all with tip 4 dot centers. Let dry. Make 232 calyxes. On waxed paper squares, pipe tip 4 cone shapes about 1/2 in. high. Make a hook in one end of wire and push into cone. Smooth with damp brush to taper around wire. Insert other end of wire into craft block and let dry. Attach drop flowers to calyxes with dots of icing; let dry. Make Base Bouquets,

Sprays and Side Sprays as indicated and assemble 9 floral cascades and 4 floral bouquets (p. 113) using floral tape. Add extra flowers if desired. Trim excess wire lengths, leaving 1³/4 in. of taped wires for inserting into dowel rods.

Ice cupcakes smooth in buttercream. Cut plastic dowel rods into 13 pieces, 1¹/4 in. long; insert in cupcakes. Position cupcakes on stand. Position flower cascades in dowel rods. Trim stems if necessary.

^Heart-Topped Tiers

PAN:	10^1/2 x 15^1/2 x 1 in. Jelly Roll
TIPS:	1, 3, 349
FONDANT:	White Ready-To-Use Rolled Fondant; Rolling Pin; Roll & Cut Mat; Round Cut-Outs™; Brush Set
RECIPE:	Buttercream Icing, p. 101
ALSO:	Heart Nesting Plastic Cookie Cutter Set; Floral Collection Flower Making Set; Meringue Powder; Gum-Tex™; Cake Board; Spatula; cornstarch, paring knife

See "Wilton Products", p. 118-127 for most Wilton items used in this project.

Several days in advance: Make heart topper. Mix 1/4 teaspoon Gum-Tex into a 2 in. ball of rolled fondant (makes 12 to 15 hearts). Roll out 1/8 in. thick; cut heart using 2nd smallest cutter from set. Let dry on cornstarch-dusted cake board. **Also:** Make flowers. Roll out fondant 1/8 in. thick; cut 10 forget-me-nots and 4 apple blossoms using cutters from Flower Making Set. Place flowers on thick foam and cup with round stick from set. Make extras to allow for breakage and let dry on cornstarch-dusted cake boards.

Cut tiers from jelly roll cake using medium and large Cut-Outs. Stack tiers. Ice smooth; cover with fondant and smooth. Pipe tip 3 bead bottom borders. For drapes, roll out fondant 1/8 in. thick; cut two 1 x 2 1/2 in. rectangles. Brush back side with water and attach drapes around cake. Attach heart to top tier. Attach flowers with dots of icing; pipe tip 1 dot centers and tip 349 leaves.

^Romance Arose

PAN:	10^1/2 x 15^1/2 x 1 in. Jelly Roll
TIPS:	2, 3
FONDANT:	White Ready-To-Use Rolled Fondant; Round Cut-Outs™; Rolling Pin; Roll & Cut Mat; Cutter/Embosser; Brush Set
RECIPE:	Buttercream Icing, p. 101
ALSO:	Confectionery Tool Set; Spatula; paring knife

See "Wilton Products", p. 118-127 for most Wilton items used in this project.

Cut tiers from jelly roll cake using medium and large Cut-Outs. Stack tiers. Ice smooth; cover with fondant and smooth. Pipe tip 3 bead bottom border; add tip 2 dots randomly on tiers. Make ribbon rose (p. 113). Trim base slightly. Attach to cake top with dots of icing.

‹ Formal Fare

PAN: Standard Muffin

RECIPE: Chocolate Buttercream, p. 101

ALSO: Shirt/Lapels and Bow Tie Patterns, p. 117; White Standard Baking Cups; Candy Melts®† in White and Light Cocoa; Parchment Triangles; Cake Board; Spatula; waxed paper, cellophane tape

See "Wilton Products", p. 118-127 for most Wilton items used in this project.

In advance: Make shirt/lapels and bow tie. Tape patterns to board; cover with waxed paper. Using melted candy in cut parchment bags, pipe in pattern areas; refrigerate until firm. Pipe dot buttons; refrigerate until firm.

Ice cupcakes smooth. Position shirt and lapels; attach bow tie with melted candy.

† Brand confectionery coating.

Initial Impressions ›

PAN: Standard Muffin

TIP: 3

COLOR: Royal Blue

RECIPES: Buttercream, Royal Icings, p. 101

ALSO: White Standard Baking Cups; Cupcake Pedestals; Meringue Powder; 10 x 14 in. Cake Board; Spatula; waxed paper

See "Wilton Products", p. 118-127 for most Wilton items used in this project.

In advance: Make monogram letters. Draw your favorite style and size of letters on cake board; cover board with waxed paper. Using royal icing, pipe tip 3 letters. Add 3/4 in. spikes on bottom of letters to insert in cupcake; let dry.

Ice cupcakes smooth. To release letters from waxed paper, carefully slide a sheet of paper underneath and lift off. Insert letters in cupcakes. Position on pedestals.

⌃ Stand Up and Cheer!

(shown on p. 4; candle cupcake instructions on p. 10)

PAN: Cookie Sheet
TIPS: 2, 2A, 3
COLORS:* Lemon Yellow, Golden Yellow, Black, Brown, Red-Red, Orange, Violet, Rose, Royal Blue, Copper (skin tone)
FONDANT: White Ready-To-Use Rolled Fondant; Rolling Pin; Roll & Cut Mat
RECIPE: Buttercream, Royal Icings, p. 101
ALSO: Party Hat, Hand Patterns, p. 114; Silly-Feet Silicone Baking Cups; 101 Cookie Cutters Set; 4 in. Lollipop Sticks; Gum-Tex™; Meringue Powder; Spatula; paring knife, waxed paper

See "Wilton Products", p. 118-127 for most Wilton items used in this project.

Two days in advance: Make heads, hands and hats. Add ¹/₂ teaspoon Gum-Tex to 4 oz. of fondant (for 4 cupcakes). Tint portions of fondant copper, yellow, orange, violet and blue. Roll out copper fondant ¹/₈ in. thick; cut heads using smallest circle cutter from 101 cutter set. Roll out remaining copper fondant and other colors ¹/₁₆ in. thick. Cut hands and hats using patterns (reverse pattern for right hand). Let dry overnight. Place heads on waxed paper and decorate using royal icing. Pipe tip 3 outline or dot eyes and pupils, dot nose, outline mouths and swirl hair. Attach hats with royal icing. Pipe tip 3 swirl pompom. Attach heads to lollipop sticks with royal icing. Let dry overnight.

Bake and cool cupcakes in silicone cups supported by cookie sheet. Cover top with a tip 2A mound; smooth with spatula. Trim lollipop sticks to 2¹/₂ in. and insert heads in cupcakes. Trim lollipop sticks to 3¹/₂ in. and insert for arms, extending 1¹/₂ in. from cupcake. Insert bag fitted with tip 2A over stick, squeeze and pull away bag to pipe arms. Attach hands at ends with royal icing. Pipe tip 3 dots or tip 2 swirls on cupcakes.

*Combine Lemon Yellow with Golden Yellow for yellow shown. Combine Brown with Red-Red for brown shown. Combine Violet with Rose for violet shown.

⌄ Skiers' Spree

(shown on p. 48)

PANS: Standard Muffin; Cookie Sheet; Cooling Grid
TIPS: 1, 2, 3, 4, 8, 16
COLORS: Orange, Christmas Red, Kelly Green, Black, Violet, Royal Blue, Lemon Yellow, Copper (skin tone)
FONDANT: White Ready-To-Use Rolled Fondant, Rolling Pin, Roll & Cut Mat, Fondant Shaping Foam
RECIPES: Buttercream, Royal Icings, p. 101; Roll-Out Cookie, p. 103
ALSO: White Standard Baking Cups; Jumbo Nonpareils Sprinkle Decorations; Large Cupcakes 'N More® Dessert Stand (holds 38); Fine Tip Primary Colors FoodWriter™ Edible Color Markers; White Sparkling Sugar; Gingerbread Boys Nesting Cutter Set; Meringue Powder; Rolling Pin; Spatula; striped gum, uncooked thin spaghetti, sugar ice cream cones (20), scissors, ruler, waxed paper, cornstarch

See "Wilton Products", p. 118-127 for most Wilton items used in this project.

In advance: Make trees. Using scissors, trim 8 cones to 3 in., 6 to 3¹/₂ in. and 4 to 4 in. Using royal icing, cover cones with tip 16 pull-out star branches. Position nonpareil ornaments on branches. Let dry overnight on waxed paper. **Also:** Make ski poles. Cut spaghetti into 1¹/₄ in. lengths. Insert in bag filled with royal icing and fitted with tip 4. Squeeze bag as you pull out spaghetti; let dry on waxed paper.

Reserve 8 oz. of plain cookie dough; tint remainder copper. Roll out copper dough; cut 16 skiers using smallest cutter. Roll out plain dough; cut 4 snowmen using smallest cutter. Bake and cool. Pipe in skiers' jackets, boots and gloves and snowmen bodies using tip 3 and royal icing (pat smooth with finger dipped in cornstarch); let dry. Draw eyes and mouth on skiers using black FoodWriter. Place cookies on waxed paper. Outline and pipe in tip 8 hats using full-strength royal icing. Pipe tip 2 swirl fur trim and pompom on skiers' hats. On all cookies, pipe tip 2 dot buttons; add tip 2 pull-out nose and tip 1 dot eyes and mouth on snowmen. Pipe tip 4 scarves on all cookies; add tip 1 pull-out fringe for skiers. Let dry.

For skis, cut gum lengthwise in half; trim point at one end and curl with fingers. Attach skiers to skis with royal icing; let dry. Ice cupcakes smooth in buttercream. Position trees, skiers and snowmen. Attach ski poles with dots of icing. Position cupcakes on stand.

Noisy Newborns

(shown on p. 71)

PANS: Jumbo Muffin; Cookie Sheet, Cooling Grid
TIPS: 2, 3, 4, 5, 7
COLORS: Copper (skin tone), Rose, Black
RECIPES: Buttercream, Royal Icings, p. 101; Roll-Out Cookie, p. 103
ALSO: Face and Hair Curl Patterns, p. 116; White Jumbo Baking Cups; Round, Oval Cut-Outs™; Rolling Pin; Meringue Powder; Spatula; $1/8$ in. wide pink satin ribbon (6 in. for each bow), waxed paper, cornstarch

See "Wilton Products", p. 118-127 for most Wilton items used in this project.

In advance: Make hair curls. Cover pattern with waxed paper; pipe tip 3 curl in royal icing. Let dry.

Roll out dough and cut face cookies using largest round Cut-Out; cut feet using medium oval Cut-Outs. Bake and cool. Ice smooth in royal icing. Place cookies on waxed paper for decorating in royal icing. Pipe tip 5 ears. Following face pattern, pipe tip 2 outline mouth. Add tip 3 dot cheeks, nose and eyes (smooth with finger dipped in cornstarch). Pipe tip 4 dot toes. Let dry. Ice cupcakes smooth in buttercream, with white diaper area and copper body area. Pipe tip 7 pull-out ties on diaper. Build up arms with tip 7; add tip 7 pull-out fingers (pat smooth). Pipe a mound of icing at top of cupcake to support head and at bottom to support feet; position head and feet. Attach hair curl with dot of royal icing. For girl, make bow; attach with royal icing.

Baby Steps

(shown on p. 71)

PANS: Standard Muffin
TIPS: 3, 8, 12
COLORS: Rose, Royal Blue
FONDANT: White Ready-To-Use Rolled Fondant; Rolling Pin; Roll & Cut Mat; Oval Cut-Outs™
RECIPE: Buttercream Icing, p. 101
ALSO: Pastel Standard Baking Cups; Spatula; craft knife, cornstarch

See "Wilton Products", p. 118-127 for most Wilton items used in this project.

Ice cupcakes smooth. Tint fondant rose or blue; roll out $1/8$ in. thick. Using medium oval Cut-Out, cut feet; trim out a small curve on one side for arch area. Position on cupcake. Use narrow end of tips, dipped in cornstarch, to cut toes; use tip 12 for big toe, tip 8 for 3 middle toes and tip 3 for small toe. Position toes.

Group Wedding

(shown on p. 85)

PANS: Standard Muffin; Cookie Sheet, Cooling Grid
TIPS: 1, 2, 13, 107, 225, 349
COLORS:* Rose, Black, Brown, Red-Red, Copper (skin tone), Kelly Green
FONDANT: White Ready-To-Use Rolled Fondant; Rolling Pin; Roll & Cut Mat; Brush Set; Cutter/Embosser
RECIPES: Buttercream, Royal Icings, p. 101; Roll-Out Cookie, p. 103
ALSO: Veil Pattern, p. 117; White Standard Baking Cups; Large Cupcakes 'N More® Dessert Stand (holds 38); Holiday Mini Cookie Cutter Set; 10 x 14 in. Cake Boards; Meringue Powder; Spatula; cornstarch, waxed paper, paring knife, ruler

See "Wilton Products", p. 118-127 for most Wilton items used in this project.

In advance: Make flowers on waxed paper-covered cake boards using royal icing. Pipe approximately 38 tip 225 drop flowers with tip 1 dot centers for bridal bouquets and 190 tip 107 drop flowers with tip 2 dot centers for garlands on cupcakes. Make extras of all to allow for breakage and let dry.

Tint cookie dough light copper; roll out and cut at least 76 cookies using mini gingerbread boy cutter. Bake and cool. Place on waxed paper-covered board and decorate using royal icing. For bride, outline and pipe in bodice using tip 2 (pat smooth with finger dipped in cornstarch). Pipe tip 2 zigzag skirt; lightly blend together zigzag lines with damp brush. Pipe tip 1 bead neckline, tip 2 swirl hair. Using black icing color thinned with water, paint eyes and mouth. Attach tip 225 drop flower in hand area with dots of icing; pipe tip 349 leaves. Roll out white fondant $1/8$ in. thick. Using pattern, cut veils and reserve remaining fondant. Position on waxed paper-covered board. Edge curve of veil with tip 2 line of icing; position bride cookie. Pipe tip 13 stars on top of head; let dry. For groom, paint eyes and mouth and add tip 2 swirl hair as for bride. Outline and pipe in tip 2 shirt (pat smooth with finger dipped in cornstarch). Outline and pipe in tip 2 jacket and pants (pat smooth); overpipe tip 2 lapels. Pipe tip 2 shoes using heavy pressure; pipe in tip 1 bow tie and dot flower. Let dry.

Ice cupcakes smooth in buttercream; mark in 5ths. Tint remaining fondant rose. Roll out $1/16$ in. thick. Using Cutter/Embosser, cut five $2^{1/2}$ x $1/8$ in. strips for each cupcake; twist and attach at markings $5/8$ in. from bottom of cupcake. Trim off excess as needed. Attach tip 107 drop flowers at garland points. Insert cookies in cupcakes. Position cupcakes on stand.

* Combine Brown with Red-Red for brown shown.

Recipes from the Wilton Kitchen

Cupcakes didn't get to be the hottest treat on the planet with good looks alone. They have to taste great too! In this section, you'll discover many of our new favorite flavors in cupcakes, fillings, and icings. Of course, you'll find delicious traditional recipes as well—lemon cupcakes and German chocolate mini cakes, classic buttercream icing, and a rich pastry cream filling. Give some of our new tastes a try. You'll love surprising family and guests with a tiramisu or key lime cupcake, or adding fun to yellow cupcakes with mocha buttercream or praline filling. Be adventurous!

Cupcake Recipes

German Chocolate Cupcakes

2 1/4 cups all-purpose flour
3/4 teaspoon baking soda
3/4 teaspoon baking powder
1/4 teaspoon salt
3/4 cup (1 1/2 sticks) unsalted butter, softened
1 1/2 cups granulated sugar
3 eggs
6 ounces German sweet chocolate, melted
1 1/2 teaspoons Wilton Clear Vanilla Extract
1 1/2 cups buttermilk

Preheat oven to 350°F. Line standard muffin pan with baking cups.

In medium bowl combine flour, baking soda, baking powder and salt. In large bowl, beat butter and sugar with electric mixer until light and fluffy. Add eggs; mix well. Add chocolate and vanilla; beat until well blended. Add dry ingredients in thirds alternating with buttermilk, beating after each addition until smooth. Spoon into baking cups. Bake 18-20 minutes or until toothpick inserted comes out clean. Cool cupcakes in pan on cooling rack for 5-8 minutes. Remove cupcakes from pan; cool completely.
Makes about 24 standard cupcakes or 5 Mini Tasty-Fill cakes.*

Cappuccino Cupcakes

1 package (18.25 oz.) white cake mix (no pudding in mix)
1 1/3 cups double-strength coffee
3 eggs
1/3 cup vegetable oil

Preheat oven to 350°F. Line standard muffin pan with baking cups.

In large bowl, combine cake mix, coffee, eggs and oil; beat with electric mixer 2 minutes. Spoon into baking cups. Bake 18-20 minutes or until toothpick inserted comes out clean. Cool cupcakes in pan on cooling rack for 5-8 minutes. Remove cupcakes from pan; cool completely.
Makes about 24 standard cupcakes or 5 Mini Tasty-Fill cakes.*

German Chocolate Mini Cake with Chocolate Ganache and Easy Cream Filling

Marble Cupcakes

1 package (18.25 oz.) yellow cake mix
  (no pudding in mix)

1 1/3 cups water

3 eggs

1/3 cup vegetable oil

2 squares (2 oz.) semi-sweet chocolate, melted

Preheat oven to 350°F. Line standard muffin pan with baking cups.

In large bowl, combine cake mix, water, eggs and oil; beat with electric mixer 2 minutes. Remove 1/2 cup batter to small bowl, mix with melted chocolate and set aside.

Fill baking cups half full with yellow batter. Top with 1 teaspoon chocolate batter; swirl with toothpick. Repeat to fill cup 2/3 full. Bake 18-20 minutes or until toothpick inserted in center comes out clean. Cool cupcakes in pan on cooling rack for 5-8 minutes. Remove cupcakes from pan; cool completely. **Makes about 24 standard cupcakes or 5 Mini Tasty-Fill cakes.***

Champagne Cupcakes

1 package (18.25 oz.) white cake mix
  (no pudding in mix)

1 1/3 cups champagne or sparkling white
    grape juice

3 egg whites

1/3 cup vegetable oil

1 tablespoon grated orange zest

Preheat oven to 350°F. Line standard muffin pan with baking cups.

In large bowl, combine cake mix, champagne (or juice), egg whites, oil and zest; beat with electric mixer 2 minutes. Spoon into baking cups. Bake 18-20 minutes or until toothpick inserted comes out clean. Cool cupcakes in pan on cooling rack for 5-8 minutes. Remove cupcakes from pan; cool completely. **Makes about 24 standard cupcakes or 5 Mini Tasty-Fill cakes.***

Butter Pecan Cupcakes

1 package (18.25 oz.) yellow cake mix
  (no pudding in mix)

1 1/3 cups water

3 eggs

1/3 cup vegetable oil

1 tablespoon Wilton No-Color Butter Flavor

1 cup chopped pecans

Preheat oven to 350°F. Line standard muffin pan with baking cups.

In large bowl, combine cake mix, water, eggs, oil and butter flavor; beat with electric mixer 2 minutes. Fold in pecans. Spoon into baking cups. Bake 18-20 minutes or until toothpick

inserted in center comes out clean. Cool cupcakes in pan on cooling rack for 5-8 minutes. Remove cupcakes from pan; cool completely. **Makes about 24 standard cupcakes or 5 Mini Tasty-Fill cakes.***

Applesauce Cinnamon Cupcakes

2 1/2 cups all-purpose flour

1 1/2 teaspoons baking powder

1 teaspoon ground cinnamon

1/2 teaspoon salt

1/4 teaspoon ground cloves

1/2 cup (1 stick) butter or margarine,
    softened

1 cup granulated sugar

2 eggs

1 jar (16 oz.) sweetened applesauce

1 cup raisins

1 cup walnuts, chopped

Preheat oven to 350°F. Line standard muffin pan with baking cups.

In medium bowl, combine flour, baking powder, cinnamon, salt and cloves; set aside. In large bowl, cream butter and sugar with electric mixer until light and fluffy. Add eggs; mix until well combined. Add flour mixture and applesauce alternately to batter; mix well. Stir in raisins and nuts. Spoon into baking cups. Bake 20-25 minutes or until toothpick inserted comes out clean. Cool cupcakes in pan on cooling rack 5-8 minutes. Remove from pan; cool completely. **Makes 18-20 standard cupcakes or 4 Mini Tasty-Fill cakes.***

Coconut Cupcakes

1 package (18.25 oz.) white cake mix
  (no pudding in mix)

1 1/3 cups water

3 eggs

1/3 cup vegetable oil

1 teaspoon coconut extract

1 cup flaked or shredded coconut

Preheat oven to 350°F. Line standard muffin pan with baking cups.

In large bowl, combine cake mix, water, eggs, oil and coconut extract; beat with electric mixer 2 minutes. Fold in shredded coconut. Spoon into baking cups. Bake 18-20 minutes or until toothpick inserted in center comes out clean. Cool cupcakes in pan on cooling rack for 5-8 minutes. Remove cupcakes from pan; cool completely. **Makes about 24 standard cupcakes or 5 Mini Tasty-Fill cakes.***

**Carrot Cupcakes with
Cream Cheese Icing**

Carrot Cupcakes

2 cups all-purpose flour

2 cups granulated sugar

2 teaspoons ground cinnamon

2 teaspoons baking soda

4 eggs

1 cup vegetable oil

4 cups freshly shredded carrots** (approx. 1 lb.)

2/3 cup chopped nuts

**Do not use pre-shredded carrots.

Preheat oven to 350°F. Line standard muffin pan with baking cups.

In medium bowl, combine flour, sugar, cinnamon and baking soda; mix well. In large bowl, beat eggs with electric mixer until foamy; add oil in a thin stream and beat well. Add flour mixture to egg mixture; mix well. Fold in carrots and nuts. Spoon into baking cups. Bake 18-20 minutes or until toothpick inserted in center comes out clean. Cool cupcakes in pan on cooling rack for 5-8 minutes. Remove cupcakes from pan; cool completely. **Makes about 2 1/2 dozen standard cupcakes or 8 Mini Tasty-Fill cakes.***

*Any of our cupcake recipes may be prepared in our Mini Tasty-Fill pans. Spray pans with vegetable pan spray, then fill each with about 1/2 cup batter. Place pans on cookie sheet and bake 14-16 minutes. Cool in pan on cooling grid for about 8 minutes; remove from pan and cool completely before filling and icing.

S'mores Cupcakes

1 package (18.25 oz.) chocolate cake mix
  (no pudding in mix)
1 1/3 cups water
3 eggs
1/3 cup vegetable oil
1 cup mini marshmallows
1 cup graham crackers, broken into
  bite-size pieces

Preheat oven to 350°F. Line standard muffin pan with baking cups.

In large bowl, combine cake mix, water, eggs and oil; beat with electric mixer 2 minutes. Spoon batter into baking cups, filling halfway. Sprinkle about 3 marshmallows and 3 graham cracker pieces in center. Cover with additional batter, filling cups 2/3 full. Bake 18-20 minutes, or until toothpick inserted in center comes out clean. Cool cupcakes in pan on cooling rack for 5-8 minutes. Remove cupcakes from pan; cool completely.

Makes about 24 standard cupcakes or 5 Mini Tasty-Fill cakes.*

Berry-Licious Cupcakes

1 package (18.25 oz.) white cake mix
  (no pudding in mix)
1 package (16 oz.) frozen raspberries or
  strawberries in sugar or syrup, thawed
Water
3 egg whites
2 tablespoons vegetable oil

Preheat oven to 350°F. Line standard muffin pan with baking cups.

Drain berries, reserving liquid. Add enough water to reserved berry liquid to make 1 1/3 cups. In large bowl, combine cake mix, berry liquid, egg whites and oil; beat with electric mixer 2 minutes. Fold in thawed berries. Spoon into baking cups. Bake 18-20 minutes or until golden. Cool cupcakes in pan on cooling rack for 5-8 minutes. Remove cupcakes from pan; cool completely.

Makes about 24 cupcakes or 5 Mini Tasty-Fill cakes.*

Peanut Butter Cupcakes

2 cups all-purpose flour
2 teaspoons baking powder
1/4 teaspoon salt
6 tablespoons butter, softened
1 1/4 cups firmly packed light brown sugar
3/4 cup peanut butter
2 eggs
1 teaspoon Wilton Clear Vanilla Extract
1 cup milk

Preheat oven to 350°F. Line standard muffin pan with baking cups.

In medium bowl, combine flour, baking powder and salt; set aside. In large bowl, cream butter, sugar and peanut butter with electric mixer until smooth. Add eggs and vanilla; mix well. Alternately add flour mixture and milk to butter mixture; mix well. Spoon into baking cups. Bake 22-24 minutes or until toothpick inserted comes out clean. Cool cupcakes in pan on cooling rack for 5-8 minutes. Remove cupcakes from pan; cool completely.

Makes about 20 standard cupcakes or 4 Mini Tasty-Fill cakes.*

Pumpkin Cupcakes

1 package (18.25 oz.) yellow cake mix
  (no pudding in the mix)
1/2 teaspoon ground cinnamon
1/4 teaspoon ground nutmeg
1 1/4 cups water
2 tablespoons vegetable oil
3 eggs
3/4 cup canned pumpkin

Preheat oven to 350°F. Line standard muffin pan with baking cups.

In large bowl, combine cake mix, cinnamon, and nutmeg. Add water, oil and eggs; beat with electric mixer 2 minutes. Add pumpkin; mix until well blended. Spoon into baking cups. Bake 25-30 minutes or until toothpick inserted in center comes out clean. Allow cupcakes to cool in pan on cooling rack for 5-8 minutes. Remove cupcakes from pan; cool completely.

Makes about 24 standard cupcakes or 5 Mini Tasty-Fill cakes.*

Berry-Licious Mini Cake with Strawberry Filling and Strawberry Buttercream Icing

Dulce de Leche Cupcakes

1 package (18.25 oz.) yellow cake mix
(no pudding in mix)
1 1/3 cups water
3 eggs
1/3 cup vegetable oil
1/2 cup caramel ice cream topping

Preheat oven to 350°F. Line standard muffin pan with baking cups.

In large bowl, combine cake mix, water, eggs and oil; beat with electric mixer 2 minutes. Fold caramel topping into batter. Spoon into baking cups. Bake 18-20 minutes or until toothpick inserted in center comes out clean. Cool cupcakes in pan on cooling rack for 5-8 minutes. Remove cupcakes from pan; cool completely.
Makes about 24 standard cupcakes or 5 Mini Tasty-Fill cakes.*

Key Lime Cupcakes

1 package (18.25 oz.) yellow cake mix
(no pudding in mix)
1 1/4 cups water
3 eggs
1/3 cup vegetable oil
2 tablespoons Key Lime juice
(about 10 Key Limes)

How to Perk Up Your Cupcake Mix

It's easy to add your own personal touch to cupcakes made with your favorite cake mix:

- Substitute frozen juice concentrate for all or part of the water used;

- Add 1/2 to 1 teaspoon almond, coconut, lemon or other favorite extract or flavoring;

- Add a few drops of concentrated candy flavor.

Once you've made the batter, stir in:

- 1/4 cup sprinkles or jimmies;

- 1/2 cup chocolate, butterscotch or peanut butter chips;

- 1/2 cup chopped nuts or shredded coconut;

- 1/2 cup chopped chocolate candy bars;

- 2 teaspoons freshly grated orange, lemon or lime zest;

- 1/2 cup mini gum drops (or chop big ones!);

- 1/4 cup crushed hard candy;

- Raisins or chopped dried fruit

Most cake mixes make between 5 and 5 1/4 cups of batter, so you can also try these "add-ins" with your favorite "from scratch" recipe.

Preheat oven to 350°F. Line standard muffin pan with baking cups.

In large bowl, combine cake mix, water, eggs, oil and lime juice; beat with electric mixer 2 minutes. Spoon into baking cups. Bake 18-20 minutes or until toothpick inserted in center comes out clean. Cool cupcakes in pan on cooling rack for 5-8 minutes. Remove from pan; cool completely.
Makes about 24 standard cupcakes or 5 Mini Tasty-Fill cakes.*

Green Tea Cupcakes

1 2/3 cups boiling water
6 green tea bags
1 package (18.25 oz.) white cake mix
(no pudding in mix)
3 egg whites
1/3 cup vegetable oil

Preheat oven to 350°F. Line standard muffin pan with baking cups.

Combine hot water and tea bags; let steep 5 minutes. Remove bags; cool to room temperature. In large bowl, combine cake mix, brewed tea, egg whites and oil; beat with electric mixer 2 minutes. Spoon into baking cups. Bake 18-20 minutes or until toothpick inserted comes out clean. Cool cupcakes in pan on cooling rack for 5-8 minutes. Remove cupcakes from pan; cool completely.
Makes about 24 standard cupcakes or 5 Mini Tasty-Fill cakes.*

Mocha Cupcakes

2 tablespoons instant coffee
1 cup warm water
1/2 cup (1 stick) butter, at room temperature
2 cups granulated sugar
4 eggs
6 ounces unsweetened chocolate, melted
1 tablespoon Wilton Clear Vanilla Extract
2 cups all-purpose flour
1 teaspoon baking soda
1 teaspoon salt

Preheat oven to 350°F. Line standard muffin pan with baking cups. Combine instant coffee and water; mix well and set aside.

In large bowl, cream butter and sugar with electric mixer until light and fluffy. Add eggs, one at a time; mix well. Add melted chocolate, vanilla and coffee mixture; mix well. Combine flour, baking soda and salt. Slowly add to butter mixture; mix well. Spoon into baking cups. Bake 18-20 minutes or until center of cupcake springs back when lightly touched. Cool cupcakes in pan on cooling rack 5-8 minutes. Remove cupcakes from pan; cool completely.
Makes about 24 standard cupcakes or 5 Mini Tasty-Fill cakes.*

Tiramisu Cupcake with Mascarpone Icing

Tiramisu Cupcakes

1 package (18.25 oz.) yellow cake mix
(no pudding in mix)
1 1/3 cups double-strength coffee
3 eggs
1/3 cup vegetable oil
12 ladyfingers, cut into bite-size pieces

Preheat oven to 350°F. Line standard muffin pan with baking cups.

In large bowl, combine cake mix, coffee, eggs and oil; beat with electric mixer 2 minutes. Fold in ladyfinger pieces. Spoon into baking cups. Bake 18-20 minutes or until golden. Cool cupcakes in pan on cooling rack for 5-8 minutes. Remove cupcakes from pan; cool completely.
Makes about 24 standard cupcakes or 5 Mini Tasty-Fill cakes.*

*Any of our cupcake recipes may be prepared in our Mini Tasty-Fill pans. Spray pans with vegetable pan spray, then fill each with about 1/2 cup batter. Place pans on cookie sheet and bake 14-16 minutes. Cool in pan on cooling grid for about 8 minutes; remove from pan and cool completely before filling and icing.

Red Velvet Cupcakes

2 1/2 cups all-purpose flour

2 tablespoons cocoa powder

1 1/2 teaspoons baking powder

1 teaspoon salt

1/2 cup (1 stick) butter or margarine, softened

1 1/2 cups granulated sugar

2 eggs

1 1/2 teaspoons No-Taste Red Icing Color

1 teaspoon Wilton Clear Vanilla Extract

1 cup buttermilk

2 tablespoons water

1 1/2 teaspoons white vinegar

1 teaspoon baking soda

Preheat oven to 350°F. Line standard muffin pan with baking cups.

In medium bowl, combine flour, cocoa, baking powder and salt; set aside. In large bowl, cream butter and sugar with electric mixer until light and fluffy. Add eggs, icing color and vanilla extract; mix well until icing color is well incorporated (scraping down sides of bowl when necessary). Alternately add flour mixture and buttermilk to butter mixture; add water and mix well. In small bowl, combine white vinegar and baking soda; gently stir into cupcake mixture. Spoon into baking cups. Bake 20-22 minutes or until toothpick inserted comes out clean. Cool cupcakes in pan on cooling rack for 5-8 minutes. Remove cupcakes from pan; cool completely.

Makes about 20 standard cupcakes or 4 Mini Tasty-Fill cakes.*

White Chocolate Macadamia Nut Cupcakes

1 package (18.25 oz.) yellow cake mix

1 1/3 cups water

3 eggs

1/3 cup vegetable oil

1/3 cup coarsely chopped white chocolate

1/3 cup chopped toasted macadamia nuts

Preheat oven to 350°F. Line standard muffin pan with baking cups.

In large bowl, combine cake mix, water, eggs and oil; beat with electric mixer 2 minutes. Fold in white chocolate and macadamia nuts. Spoon into baking cups. Bake 18-20 minutes or until toothpick inserted comes out clean. Cool cupcakes in pan on cooling rack for 5-8 minutes. Remove cupcakes from pan; cool completely.

Makes about 24 standard cupcakes or 5 Mini Tasty-Fill cakes.*

Red Velvet Cupcake with Buttercream Icing

Brownie Cupcakes

1 3/4 cups all-purpose flour

1/2 teaspoon salt

4 squares (1 oz. ea.) unsweetened chocolate, chopped

1 1/2 cups (3 sticks) butter, cut into pieces

1 1/2 cups granulated sugar

4 eggs, lightly beaten

2 teaspoons Wilton Clear Vanilla Extract

2 cups pecans, chopped (optional)

Preheat oven to 350°F. Line standard muffin pan with baking cups.

In medium bowl, combine flour and salt. In small heavy saucepan or microwave-safe bowl, melt butter and chocolate; stir until blended. In large bowl, combine chocolate mixture with sugar; mix well. Whisk in eggs and vanilla. Add flour mixture to chocolate mixture; mix until blended. If desired, stir in nuts. Distribute brownie mixture evenly into baking cups. Bake 18-20 minutes or until toothpick inserted comes out clean. Cool cupcakes in pan on cooling rack for 5-8 minutes. Remove cupcakes from pan; cool completely.

Makes about 20 standard cupcakes or 4 Mini Tasty-Fill cakes.*

Lemon Cupcakes

1 package (18.25 oz.) white cake mix (no pudding in the mix)

1 1/4 cups water

2 tablespoons vegetable oil

3 egg whites

1 tablespoon grated lemon zest

1 tablespoon fresh lemon juice

Preheat oven to 350°F. Line standard muffin pan with baking cups.

In large bowl, combine cake mix, water, oil and egg whites; beat with electric mixer 2 minutes. Add lemon zest and juice; mix until well blended. Spoon into baking cups. Bake 20-22 minutes or until toothpick inserted comes out clean. Cool cupcakes in pan on cooling rack for 5-8 minutes. Remove cupcakes from pan; cool completely.

Makes about 24 standard cupcakes or 5 Mini Tasty-Fill cakes.*

*Any of our cupcake recipes may be prepared in our Mini Tasty-Fill pans. Spray pans with vegetable pan spray, then fill each with about 1/2 cup batter. Place pans on cookie sheet and bake 14-16 minutes. Cool in pan on cooling grid for about 8 minutes; remove from pan and cool completely before filling and icing.

Icing Recipes

Buttercream Icing

1/2 cup solid vegetable shortening[1]
1/2 cup (1 stick) butter, softened
1 teaspoon Wilton Clear Vanilla Extract
4 cups sifted confectioners' sugar (approx. 1 lb.)
2 tablespoons milk[2]

In large bowl, cream shortening and butter with electric mixer until light and fluffy. Add vanilla; mix well. Gradually add sugar, one cup at a time, beating well on medium speed; scrape sides and bottom of bowl often. When all sugar has been mixed in, icing will appear dry. Add milk; beat at medium speed until light and fluffy. Keep icing covered with a damp cloth until ready to use. For best results, keep icing bowl in refrigerator when not in use. Refrigerated in an airtight container, this icing can be stored 2 weeks. Re-whip before using. **Makes about 3 cups.**

[1] Substitute all-vegetable shortening and 1/2 teaspoon Wilton No-Color Butter Flavor for pure white icing and stiffer consistency.

[2] Add 2 tablespoons light corn syrup, water or milk per recipe to thin for icing cake.

Flavor Variations for Buttercream Icing or Ready-To-Use Decorator Icing

Using 3 cups buttercream or white icing:

- **Lemon:** Add 2 tablespoons lemon juice and 1 tablespoon freshly grated lemon zest to prepared icing.

- **Key Lime:** Add 2 tablespoons key lime juice and 1 tablespoon key lime zest to prepared icing.

- **Mango:** Stir 3/4 cup mango jam or preserves into prepared icing.

- **Coconut:** Add 2 1/2 teaspoons coconut extract to icing. If desired, stir 1 cup flaked or shredded coconut into prepared icing.

- **Orange:** Stir 1 tablespoon freshly grated orange zest into prepared icing.

- **Candy Cane:** Stir 3/4 cup finely crushed peppermint hard candies into prepared icing.

- **Caramel:** Add 1/2 cup caramel ice cream topping to prepared icing.

- **Cinnamon:** Stir 1 teaspoon ground cinnamon into prepared icing.

- **Strawberry or Raspberry:** Place 3/4 cup seedless strawberry or raspberry jam or preserves in bowl; stir until smooth. Stir into prepared icing.

Chocolate Buttercream Icing

To Buttercream Icing recipe: Add 3/4 cup cocoa (or three 1 oz. unsweetened chocolate squares, melted) and an additional 1 to 2 tablespoons milk. Mix until well blended.

Darker Chocolate Icing: Add 1/4 cup sifted cocoa powder (or 4 more unsweetened chocolate squares) and 1 more tablespoon milk to Chocolate Buttercream Icing.

Mocha Buttercream Icing

1/2 cup solid vegetable shortening
1/2 cup (1 stick) butter, softened
1 square (1 oz.) unsweetened chocolate, melted
1 tablespoon instant coffee
1 teaspoon Wilton Clear Vanilla Extract
4 cups sifted confectioners' sugar (approx. 1 lb.)
2 tablespoons milk

In large bowl, cream shortening and butter with electric mixer until light and fluffy. Add melted chocolate, instant coffee and vanilla; mix well. Gradually add sugar, one cup at a time, beating well on medium speed; scrape sides and bottom of bowl often. When all sugar has been mixed in, icing will appear dry. Add milk; beat at medium speed until light and fluffy. Keep icing covered with a damp cloth until ready to use. For best results, keep icing bowl in refrigerator when not in use. Refrigerated in an airtight container, this icing can be stored 2 weeks. Re-whip before using. **Makes about 3 cups.**

Royal Icing

3 tablespoons meringue powder
4 cups sifted (approx. 1 lb.) confectioners' sugar
6 tablespoons warm water

Beat all ingredients until icing forms a peak, 7-10 minutes at low speed with a heavy duty mixer, 10-12 min. at high speed with a hand-held mixer. **Makes about 3 cups.**

Cream Cheese Icing

3 packages (8 oz. ea.) cream cheese, softened
1 tablespoon orange juice
1 teaspoon finely grated orange zest
4 cups sifted confectioners' sugar

In large bowl, beat cream cheese, orange juice and zest with electric mixer until smooth. Gradually add confectioners' sugar. Continue beating until icing is smooth and creamy. Refrigerate until ready to use. **Makes about 4 cups.**

Color Flow Icing
(full-strength for outlining)

1/2 cup plus 1 teaspoon water
4 cups sifted confectioners' sugar (about 1 lb.)
2 tablespoons Color Flow Mix

With electric mixer, using grease-free utensils, blend all ingredients on low speed for 5 minutes. If using hand mixer, use high speed. Stir in desired icing color. Color flow icing "crusts" quickly, so keep bowl covered with a damp cloth while using. **Makes about 2 cups.**

Thinned Color Flow: In order to fill an outlined area, the recipe above must be thinned with 1/2 teaspoon of water per 1/4 cup of icing (just a few drops at a time as you near proper consistency). Use grease-free spoon or spatula

Peanut Butter Cupcake with Chocolate Buttercream Icing and Chocolate Pastry Cream Filling

to stir slowly. Color flow is ready for filling in outlines when a small amount dropped into the mixture takes a count of ten to disappear.

Note: Color flow designs take a long time to dry, so plan to do your color flow piece up to 1 week in advance.

Quick-Pour Fondant Icing

6 cups sifted confectioners' sugar (about 1 1/2 lbs.)
1/2 cup water
2 tablespoons light corn syrup
1 teaspoon almond extract
Wilton Icing Colors (if desired)

Cover cakes lightly with buttercream icing. Let set 15 minutes.

Place sugar in saucepan. Combine water and corn syrup. Add to sugar and stir until well-mixed. Place over low heat. Don't allow temperature of mixture to exceed 100°F. Remove from heat; stir in extract and icing color. Follow instructions for covering cupcakes on p. 106. Touch up any bare spots with spatula. Let set. Excess icing may be reheated. **Makes 2 1/2 cups.**

Mascarpone Icing

1 container (8 oz.) mascarpone cheese
1 tablespoon milk
1/2 cup confectioners' sugar

In large bowl, combine cheese, milk and sugar. Beat with mixer until ingredients are blended. Keep icing bowl in refrigerator when not in use. Refrigerate in an airtight container. After icing cupcakes, sprinkle chocolate to garnish. Refrigerate until ready to serve. **Makes about 2 cups.**

Chocolate Ganache

1 package (14 oz.) Wilton Dark Cocoa Candy Melts®, chopped
1/2 cup heavy whipping cream

In large saucepan, heat whipping cream just to boiling. (Do not boil.) Remove from heat, add chopped candy, and stir until melted and smooth. If mixture is too thick, add 1 to 2 additional tablespoons whipping cream.

Can be used as filling if allowed to thicken or can be poured on baked goods as glaze. **Makes about 2 cups.**

For Whipped Ganache: Cover and refrigerate until chilled. When ready to use, gently whip until thickened. Refrigerate until ready to serve.

Filling Recipes

Cinnamon-Sugar Cream Cheese Filling

1 package (8 oz.) cream cheese, softened
1/2 cup confectioners' sugar
1/2 teaspoon ground cinnamon
1/4 cup milk

In large bowl, combine cream cheese, sugar, cinnamon and milk. Beat with mixer until well blended. Refrigerate until ready to use. Fill cupcakes. Refrigerate until ready to serve. **Makes about 1 1/2 cups.**

Chocolate Pastry Cream Filling

6 tablespoons granulated sugar
3 tablespoons all-purpose flour
1/2 teaspoon salt
1 cup half & half
5 egg yolks
2 teaspoon Wilton Clear Vanilla Extract
3 squares (3 oz.) semi-sweet chocolate, finely chopped

In small saucepan, blend sugar, flour, salt, half

& half and egg yolks with wire whip. Stirring constantly, heat over medium heat until mixture is thickened, about 5 minutes. Remove from heat; stir in vanilla and chocolate. Continue stirring until chocolate is melted. Transfer to medium bowl; cover surface with plastic wrap to prevent skin from forming. Refrigerate 2 hours or until chilled. Stir before using. Fill cupcakes. Refrigerate until ready to serve. **Makes about 1 3/4 cups filling.**

Pastry Cream Filling

6 tablespoons granulated sugar
3 tablespoons all-purpose flour
1/2 teaspoon salt
1 cup half & half
4 egg yolks
1 teaspoon Wilton Clear Vanilla Extract

In small saucepan, blend all ingredients except vanilla with wire whip. Heat over medium heat, stirring constantly, until mixture is thickened, about 5 minutes. Remove from heat; stir in vanilla. Transfer to medium bowl; cover surface with plastic wrap to prevent skin from forming. Refrigerate 2 hours or until chilled. Stir before using. Fill cupcakes. Refrigerate until ready to serve. **Makes about 1 1/2 cups filling.**

Praline Filling

1 cup (2 sticks) unsalted butter, softened
8 egg yolks
2 cups firmly packed brown sugar
1/4 teaspoon salt
1/4 teaspoon maple flavoring
2 cups finely chopped pecans

In medium saucepan, combine butter, egg yolks, brown sugar and salt. Bring to a boil over medium heat, whisking constantly until thickened, about 10 minutes. Remove from heat; stir in flavoring and pecans. Transfer to medium bowl; cover surface with plastic wrap to prevent skin from forming. Refrigerate 2 hours or until chilled. Stir before using. Fill cupcakes. Refrigerate until ready to serve. **Makes about 2 2/3 cups filling.**

Strawberry Filling

1 package (16 oz.) frozen sliced strawberries packed in sugar, thawed
1/3 cup granulated sugar
3 tablespoons cornstarch
1 teaspoon lemon juice

Drain strawberries; reserving liquid. Add enough water to liquid to equal 1 1/4 cups. In large saucepan, combine strawberry liquid, sugar, cornstarch and lemon juice; mix well. Heat and stir until mixture boils and thickens. Cool completely. Stir strawberries into cooled

mixture. Refrigerate until ready to use. **Makes about 2 cups filling.**

For Raspberry Filling, substitute 1 package (16 oz.) frozen raspberries packed in syrup, thawed, for frozen strawberries.

For Pineapple Filling, substitute 1 can (16 oz.) crushed pineapple in syrup for frozen strawberries.

Easy Cream Filling

3/4 cup flaked coconut
1/4-1/2 cup grated or shaved semi-sweet chocolate
1 container (8 oz.) frozen whipped topping, thawed

In medium bowl, gently fold coconut and chocolate into thawed whipped topping. Refrigerate until ready to use. Fill cupcakes. Refrigerate until ready to serve. **Makes about 2 cups filling.**

Other Recipes

Thinned Fondant Adhesive

1 oz. Wilton Ready-To-Use Rolled Fondant (1 1/2 in. ball)
1/4 teaspoon water

Note: Use this mixture when attaching dried fondant to other fondant decorations or for attaching freshly cut fondant pieces to lollipop sticks or florist wire.

Knead water into fondant until it becomes softened and sticky. To attach a fondant decoration, place mixture in a cut parchment bag or brush on back of decoration. Recipe may be doubled.

Candy Clay

14 oz. pk. Candy Melts®
1/3 cup light corn syrup

Melt Candy Melts® following package directions. Add corn syrup and stir to blend. Turn out mixture onto waxed paper and let set at room temperature to dry. Wrap well and store at room temperature until needed. Candy clay handles best if hardened overnight.

To Use: Candy clay will be very hard at the start; knead a small portion at a time until workable. If candy clay gets too soft, set aside at room temperature or refrigerate briefly. When rolling out candy clay, sprinkle work surface with cornstarch or cocoa (for cocoa clay) to prevent sticking; roll to approximately 1/8 in. thick. White candy clay may be tinted using Candy Color or Icing Color. Knead in color until well-blended. Candy clay will last for several weeks at room temperature in an airtight container.

Wilton Gelatin Treats

This recipe yields a firmer gelatin, recommended for molding and cutting shapes.

2 packages (3 oz. ea.) flavored gelatin
1 1/4 cups boiling water

Completely dissolve gelatin in boiling water. Lightly spray pan or baking cups with vegetable pan spray. Slowly pour gelatin into pans or cups. Refrigerate until set, at least 3 hours. Unmold.

Jelly Roll Yellow Sponge Cake

5 medium eggs, separated
Pinch of salt
1/2 teaspoon cream of tartar
1/2 cup granulated sugar
3/4 cup sifted cake flour
3/4 teaspoon Wilton Clear Vanilla Extract

Preheat oven to 400°F. Grease jelly roll pan with 1 tablespoon shortening. Sprinkle well with cake flour, shaking off loose flour. Separate eggs; beat yolks 1 minute. Add pinch of salt to egg whites, then beat until foamy. Add cream of tartar and continue beating whites until they cling to bottom and sides of bowl, then beat 1 minute longer. Fold beaten egg yolks into egg whites gently but quickly. Fold in sugar, flour and vanilla. Do not overmix.

Pour batter into pan, spreading evenly from center out with a spoon. Tap pan several times on table to break any air bubbles and bake in center of oven 10-12 minutes. Loosen sides and bottom. Turn out of pan onto a dry towel. Cool 10 minutes, then trim crusty edges. Roll loosely in a towel and cool on rack before decorating. **Makes 5 cups batter.**

Roll-Out Cookies

1 cup (2 sticks) butter, softened
1 1/2 cups granulated sugar
1 egg
1 1/2 teaspoons vanilla extract
1/2 teaspoon almond extract
2 3/4 cups all-purpose flour
2 teaspoons baking powder
1 teaspoon salt

Preheat oven to 400°F. In large bowl, cream butter and sugar with electric mixer until light and fluffy. Add egg, vanilla and almond extracts. Mix flour, baking powder and salt; add one cup at a time to butter mixture, mixing after each addition. Do not chill dough. Divide dough into 2 balls. On floured surface, roll each ball into circle approximately 12 inches in diameter and 1/8 inch thick. Dip cutters in flour before each use. Bake cookies on an ungreased cookie sheet on top rack of oven for 6-7 minutes or until cookies are lightly browned. **Makes about 4 dozen cookies.**

Chocolate Roll-Out Cookies

3/4 cup butter or margarine, softened
1 cup granulated sugar
2 eggs
1 teaspoon vanilla extract
3 squares (1 oz. ea.) unsweetened chocolate, melted and cooled
3 cups all-purpose flour
2 teaspoons baking powder
1 teaspoon salt

Preheat oven to 375°F. In large bowl, beat together butter and sugar with mixer until light and fluffy. Add eggs and vanilla; mix well. Blend in chocolate. Combine flour and baking powder; gradually add to butter mixture, beating until smooth. Cover and chill until firm, about 1 hour. Roll out dough approximately 1/8 in. thick. Dip cookie cutter in flour before each use. Bake cookies on ungreased cookie sheet 8-10 minutes or until cookies are lightly browned. Remove to rack and cool thoroughly. **Makes about 2 dozen cookies.**

Chocolate Mousse

1 envelope unflavored gelatin
1/2 cup liquid (water, liqueur, strong coffee)
1 package (3.4 oz.) regular chocolate pudding mix (NOT INSTANT)
1 1/2 cups milk
6 squares (1 oz. ea.) bittersweet or semi-sweet chocolate
1 cup heavy whipping cream
1/2 cup confectioners' sugar

In small bowl, sprinkle gelatin over liquid; let stand until softened, about 5 minutes. Set aside. In medium saucepan, whisk together pudding mix and milk. Bring to a boil, stirring constantly; remove from heat. Add chocolate and softened gelatin; stir or whisk until smooth. Transfer to bowl; place bowl in another bowl filled with ice. Whisk until very cool and thick. Whip cream with sugar; fold into pudding mixture. Refrigerate until ready to serve. **Makes about 5 cups.**

Use the chart below to find some of our favorite pairings of cakes, icings and fillings, then create your own party cupcake sampler!

Cupcakes	Icing						Fillings					
	Buttercream	Chocolate Buttercream	Mocha	Cream Cheese	Ganache	Mascarpone	Pastry Cream	Chocolate Pastry Cream	Praline	Strawberry	Cinnamon Sugar Cream Cheese	Easy Cream Filling
Red Velvet	●						●					●
S'mores	●	●	●		●		●	●				●
Tiramisu	●				●	●						
Marble	●	●	●		●		●	●	●		●	
Peanut Butter	●	●			●		●	●			●	●
Pumpkin	●			●			●	●	●		●	
Dulce de Leche	●					●	●	●	●			
Lemon	●						●			●		●
German Chocolate		●	●		●		●					
Green Tea	●						●					
Key Lime	●						●					
Carrot	●			●			●				●	
Coconut	●						●				●	
Mocha	●	●	●				●	●	●		●	
Champagne	●						●	●				
White Chocolate Macadamia Nut	●						●					●
Berry-Licious	●	●			●		●			●		●
Applesauce Cinnamon	●	●			●		●	●	●		●	
Brownie	●	●	●		●		●					
Butter Pecan	●						●					
Cappuccino	●		●		●		●	●	●		●	

The Perfect Cupcakes
How to bake, ice and decorate

Cupcakes should be easy and fun. Like everything you serve, they should also look and taste as good as possible. You wouldn't want it any other way! In this section, you will discover the secrets to making the perfect cupcakes. Baking to a perfect height and color. Covering with colorful and delicious icings. Adding those extra decorative touches to make your cupcakes fit the occasion. Follow our kitchen-tested steps and your cupcakes will be easy, fun and beautiful!

Preparing the Pan

There are 3 easy ways to bake cupcakes, all of which will help you turn out fluffy, crumb-free cakes perfect for icing and decorating. If you are baking in a pan with a dark or non-stick surface, you should lower the recommended recipe temperature by 25°F to avoid overbrowning. Dark pans give your cakes a darker finish when baked at 350°F.

With Paper/Foil Cups
(in metal muffin pan)

Cups create a pretty fluted surface and allow you to bake without grease or pan spray. They also help keep cupcakes from drying out. Be sure to spread cups evenly in pan cavities and check that cups are level before filling. When using foil cups, remove paper liners, if included, before filling and baking; liners are included to help separate the thin foil cups.

Without Cups (in metal muffin pan)

Even non-stick pans must be prepared before baking. Prepare pan cavities by spraying with non-stick vegetable oil pan spray or Wilton Bake Easy!™. Or brush cavities with Wilton Cake Release or coat with vegetable shortening and flour for perfect release without sticking.

With Silicone Cups

We used these oven-safe flexible cups often in this book. It's easy to see how much fun they are to serve in, with their unique shapes and exciting colors; but you'll love them for baking too—they release cupcakes with ease and are dishwasher safe. We suggest preparing cups with non-stick pan spray before baking. Always place cups on a cookie sheet or sheet pan for level baking and easy removal from oven. You may need to add more baking time for some shapes. To remove cupcakes, invert cup and apply gentle pressure to the bottom while gently peeling cup away.

Preparing the Batter

As a general rule, most cake recipes or mixes will work for cupcakes. Simply adjust the baking time for the smaller portion and test by inserting a toothpick during baking. Proper measuring of ingredients is a key to perfectly baked cupcakes—especially when you're making them from scratch as with our recipes, starting on page 96. For dry ingredients, spoon into nesting measuring cups, overfilling the top. Level by running a spatula along the top. For wet ingredients, use glass measuring cups. Pour to the exact level needed.

Filling Cups with Batter

For a consistent size, fill cups $1/2$ to $2/3$ full. The best way we've found to add the batter is to squeeze it into the cup using a decorating bag. Just fill the bag about halfway with batter, and squeeze perfect portions into your cups. Using a bag will give you better control, especially when making mini cupcakes. The bag keeps batter from spilling over the cavities. Other good ways to fill—use an ice cream scoop, a large spoon or a measuring cup.

Adding Mix-Ins to Batter

Bake delicious flavors and textures right into your cupcakes! After mixing the batter, just before filling the cups, gently fold in jimmies, sprinkles, chopped nuts, crushed hard candy or fruit. It's an easy way to perk up any cupcakes made from a mix.

Foolproof Baking

Baking a perfect cupcake for decorating is much the same as baking a perfect full-size cake. You want to avoid high or misshapen crowns, dark brown surfaces and burned bottoms. First, know your oven. Actual oven temperatures can vary greatly from the temperature you set, so check periodically with an oven thermometer. For dark or non-stick bakeware, we suggest setting the oven at 25° less than stated in recipe. Bake cupcakes on the middle rack of your oven and make sure the rack is level. If you are baking in several pans at the same time, you may need to add a few minutes to baking time. Test for doneness a few minutes before baking time ends—insert a toothpick in the center of cupcake. If toothpick comes out clean, cupcakes are done. For most recipes in this book, baking time is 18 to 20 minutes.

Filled Centers

You can really have fun with flavor when you add a tasty filling to your baked cupcakes. Flavored whipped cream, chocolate or fruit work especially well—you can find great recipes for Mocha, Praline, Vanilla Pastry Cream Fillings and more on page 102. Filling the centers is easy using the Bismarck tip 230, available in our Cupcake Decorating Set.

Prepare a decorating bag with your selected filling and tip 230; insert tip in top center of an uniced cupcake and squeeze out a small amount of filling. Or, use the Wilton Dessert Decorator, which includes a filling tip and an easy-to-control cylinder for adding just the right amount. For a delicious filling you can add before baking cupcakes, try candy!

Covering the Cupcake

You can be as fancy as you want when covering your cupcakes. Just do it neatly, for treats that look even more tempting! Use one of the easy methods below to serve cupcakes with a professional look. Or, try dipping cupcakes in melted icing, then topping with sprinkles.

Using Buttercream with a Spatula

The traditional way to ice cupcakes, neatly and quickly.

1. Place a dollop of icing at the center of the cupcake.

2. Spread icing across the top, pushing toward the edges. For a smooth look, run the spatula edge across the top.

For a fluffier look, lightly touch the iced surface with the spatula blade and lift up.

Using Buttercream with Tip 1M Swirls

Add a fancier flourish with an elegant spiral of icing. Star tip 1M creates pretty texture everyone will love.

1. Hold tip 1M at a 90° angle to cupcake surface. Pipe a spiral of icing, beginning at the outer edge and

working inward. Stop pressure; pull tip away.

2. Pipe a second spiral on top. End spiral at center. Stop pressure; pull tip away.

Using Rolled Fondant

Fondant gives your cupcakes a silky-smooth surface, perfect for displaying icing flowers, figure piping and other decorations. The formula for covering cupcakes or mini cakes completely with rolled fondant is the same as for covering cakes. Measure opposite sides and the top of cake (baked without baking cups) across the center. Roll out fondant to that size, 1/8 in. thick. For example, a standard 2 in. wide cupcake, with two sides each 1½ in. high, equals 5 in. diameter. It is easier to cover a cupcake bottom side up.

1. Lightly ice cupcake using a spatula.

2. Roll out fondant 1/8 in. thick to desired size.

3. Cover cupcake with fondant. Trim off excess fondant at base with spatula.

4. Smooth fondant around cupcake with your fingers.

Covering the Cupcake (cont.)
Using Ganache, Candy Melts®†
or Poured Icings

You can't go wrong with any of these delicious coatings. Each will give cupcakes, mini cakes and other baked goods a beautiful finish—choose the look you want for your event.

Ganache combines our Candy Melts with whipping cream to create a rich chocolate coating with a satiny look. It adds a creamy texture and satiny finish to treats. Coating with **Candy Melts** alone will help treats set up firmer than icings or ganache. Candy is perfect for kids' treats because it's shiny, colorful, easy to handle and eat. **Poured Icings**, like thinned buttercream or poured fondant, give you the most color versatility and a smooth finish. You can tint these icings in virtually any shade.

† Brand confectionery coating.

1. Place cooled cupcakes or mini cakes on cooling grid positioned over cookie sheet or pan. Cupcakes which will be covered completely should be turned bottom side up. If using Candy Melts, melt following package directions. If using icing, follow recipe directions to reach pouring consistency.

2. Pour ganache, candy or icing on center of cupcake using pan or measuring cup. Or, pipe candy or icing from a cut decorating bag. Cover the cupcake completely, or use your coating as a glaze to simply cover tops and drip over the sides.

3. Let set.

Decorating with a Bag and Tip

Preparing the Bag
Decorating bags hold the icing and decorating tip so you can create a variety of decorations.

Correct Bag Position
The way your decorations curl, point and lie depends not only on icing consistency but also on the way you hold the bag and the way you move it. Bag positions are described in terms of both angle and direction.

Angle
Angle refers to the position of the bag relative to the work surface. There are two basic angle positions, 90° (straight up) and 45° (halfway between vertical and horizontal).

90° angle or straight up, perpendicular to the surface.

45° angle or halfway between vertical and horizontal.

Direction
The angle in relation to the work surface is only half the story on bag position. The other half is the direction in which the back of the bag is pointed. Correct bag direction is easiest to learn when you think of the back of the bag as the hour hand of a clock.

When you hold the bag at a 45° angle to the surface, you can sweep out a circle with the back end of the bag by rolling your wrist and holding the end of the tip in the same spot. Pretend the circle you formed in the air is a clock face. The hours on the clock face correspond to the direction you point the back end of the bag.

The technique instructions in this Decorating Guide will list the correct direction for holding the bag. When the bag direction differs for left-handed decorators, that direction will be listed in parentheses. For example, when a bag is to be held at 3:00 for a right-handed decorator, it should be held at 9:00 for a left-handed decorator.

Back of bag at 3:00

Back of bag at 6:00

One more thing…since most decorating tip openings are the same shape all the way around, there's no right side and wrong side up when you're squeezing icing out of them. However, some tips, such as petal, ruffle, basketweave and leaf have irregularly shaped openings. For those you must watch your tip position as well as your bag position. If the tip opening must be in a special position, the instructions will tell you.

Pressure Control
In addition to having the proper icing consistency and the correct bag position, you'll need to master three types of pressure control: heavy, medium and light. The size and uniformity of your icing designs are affected by the amount of pressure you apply to the bag and the steadiness of that pressure. (In other words, how you squeeze and relax your grip on the decorating bag.) Your goal is to learn to apply pressure so consistently that you can move the bag in a free and easy glide while just the right amount of icing flows through the tip. Practice will help you achieve this control.

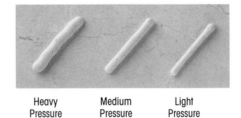

| Heavy Pressure | Medium Pressure | Light Pressure |

Tip Techniques

Decorate with Buttercream Icing unless otherwise noted.

Ball

A ball is the first step to learn for figure piping and is an essential technique for borders. Use the same basic steps to make dots.

Practice With: Tip 3

Icing Consistency: Medium

Bag Position: 90° (straight up)

Hold Tip: Slightly above surface

1. Squeeze the bag, applying steady even pressure. As the icing begins to build up, raise the tip with it, but keep the tip end buried in the icing.

2. Stop squeezing as you bring the end of the tip to the surface.

3. Lift the tip up and pull away from your piped ball. Use the edge of the tip to shave off any point so that your ball is nicely rounded.

Bead

A pretty border decoration, which uses a shell motion. To make a bead heart, pipe one bead, then a second, joining the tails. Smooth together using a decorator brush.

Practice With: Tip 5

Icing Consistency: Medium

Bag Position: 45° at 3:00 (9:00 for lefties)

Hold Tip: Slightly above surface

1. Squeeze as you lift tip slightly so that icing fans out.

2. Relax pressure as you draw the tip down and bring bead to a point.

3. To make a bead border, start the end of your next bead so that the fanned end covers the tail of the preceding bead to form an even chain.

Ruffle

Everyone loves a ruffle's graceful motion—ruffles always add interest to a cupcake. Use them as a border or to trim dresses or baby bonnets.

Practice With: Tip 104

Icing Consistency: Medium

Bag Position: 45° at 3:00 (9:00)

Hold Tip: Wide end lightly touching surface with narrow end facing down and away from surface

  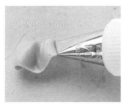 

1. With tip in position, move wrist up to pull up icing.

2. Move wrist down to complete one curl of the ruffle.

3. Repeat up and down motion.

4. Raise and lower the narrow end as you move around the cupcake. Repeat this motion for the entire ruffle.

Star

The star is one of the easiest decorations to master—essential for filling in outlined areas and borders.

Practice With: Tip 16

Icing Consistency: Medium

Bag Position: 90° (straight up)

Hold Tip: Between 1/8 and 1/4 in. above surface

1. Hold bag in position with one hand while your other hand holds the tip steady. Squeeze bag to form a star. Increasing or decreasing the pressure changes the size of the star.

2. Stop squeezing the bag completely before you lift the tip from the star.

3. Lift the tip up and pull away from piped star.

Pull-Out Star

Pull-out stars add more dimension to your cupcake. They stand up and away from the surface for a look that gets attention! Great for hair, pompom and fur effects.

Practice With: Tip 16

Icing Consistency: Medium

Bag Position: 45°

Hold Tip: Between 1/8 and 1/4 in. above surface

1. As you squeeze out icing, pull tip up and away from cupcake.

2. Stop pressure and pull away. Work from the bottom to the top of area to be covered with pull-out stars.

Outline

Characters or designs are often outlined first, then piped in with stars or zigzags.

Practice With: Tip 3

Icing Consistency: Thin

Bag Position: 45° at 3:00 (9:00)

Hold Tip: Slightly above surface

  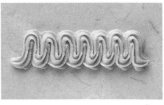

1. Touch tip to surface. Raise the tip slightly and continue to squeeze.

2. The icing will flow out of the tip while you direct it along the surface.

3. To end, stop squeezing, touch tip to surface and pull away.

Zigzag

A quick way to fill in outlined areas, great for sweater and cuff effects, hat brims and more.

Practice With: Tip 16

Icing Consistency: Medium

Bag Position: 45° at 3:00 (9:00)

Hold Tip: Lightly touching surface

1. Steadily squeeze and move your hand in a tight up and down position.

2. Continue piping up and down with steady pressure. To end, stop

pressure and pull tip away. For more elongated zigzags, move your hand to the desired height while maintaining a steady pressure. For a more relaxed

look, increase the width as you move the bag along.

3. Repeat as you move in a straight line with consistent up/down motion.

Swirl Drop Flowers

The swirled look adds a nice motion effect to the cake. You must squeeze and turn at the same time.

Practice With: Tips 2D, 3

Icing Consistency: Medium Buttercream or Royal Icing

Bag Position: 90° (straight up)

Hold Tip: For flower, lightly touching surface; for center, slightly above flower

1. Turn your wrist in toward you before piping. Hold bag straight up, just touching the surface. You will turn wrist a full twist, starting with the flat of your knuckles at 3:00 (9:00 for

left-handers). As you squeeze out the icing, slowly turn your hand, with knuckles ending at 12:00.

2. Stop squeezing and lift the tip away.

3. Make a tip 3 dot flower center, holding your bag straight up and keeping the tip buried as you squeeze. Stop squeezing, then pull your tip up and away.

Daisy

Make these perky spring flowers in advance—they're a great way to top fresh cupcakes. Highlight centers with Cake Sparkles or Colored Sugar.

Practice With: Tips 104, 5

Icing Consistency: Medium Royal Icing

Bag Position: For petals, 45° at 3:00 (9:00 for left-handers); for center, 90° (straight up)

Hold Tip: For petals, wide end lightly touching ¼ in. away from center of nail, narrow end pointing out to outer edge; for center, hold slightly above flower

Flower Nail: No. 7

1. Dot center of flower nail with icing as a guide for flower center. Starting at any point near outer edge of nail, squeeze and move tip towards center icing dot. Stop pressure, pull tip away.

2. Repeat for a total of 12 or more petals.

3. Add tip 5 flower center and press to flatten. For pollen effect, dampen your fingertip, dip in crushed Cake Sparkles or Colored Sugar, then press on center.

Wild Rose

A pretty year-round flower piped about the size of a flower nail. If you prefer a more cupped shape, increase the angle of the tip. Dry in Flower Formers (p. 126)

Practice With: Tips 103, 5

Icing Consistency: Medium Royal Icing

Bag Position: For petals, 45° at 3:00 (9:00); for center 90°

Hold Tip: For petals, wide end lightly touching center of nail, narrow end pointing out and raised ⅛ in. above nail surface; for centers, slightly above flower

Flower Nail: #7

1. Use tip 103 at a 45° angle. Touch nail with wide end of tip, keeping narrow end just slightly above nail surface. Begin at center of flower nail and squeeze out first petal, turning nail ⅕ turn as you move tip out toward

edge of nail. Relax pressure as you return to center of nail, curving tip slightly upward to create a cupped shape. Stop squeezing as wide end touches center of nail and lift up.

2. Repeat step 4 more times.

3. Pipe tip 5 flower center and press to flatten. For pollen effect, dampen your fingertip, dip in sugar, then press on center.

The Wilton Rose

NOTE: If you are going to be placing your roses on your cake immediately, waxed paper squares are not needed. To remove finished roses, use the Wilton Flower Lifter. Slide flower from lifter onto cake, using a spatula.

Practice With: Tips 104, 12

Icing Consistency: Royal or Stiff Buttercream

Bag Position: Base 90° (straight up); petals 45° at 4:30 (7:30)

Hold Tip: For base, slightly above nail; for petals, wide end touching base

Flower Nail: #7

1. Make the rose base, using tip 12 and flower nail #7. Hold the bag straight up, the end of tip 12 slightly above the center of your waxed paper-covered flower nail, which is held in your other hand. Using heavy pressure, build up a base, remembering to keep your tip buried as you squeeze. Start to lift the tip higher, gradually raise the tip, and decrease the pressure.

2. Stop pressure, pull up and lift away. The rose base should be 1 1/2 times as high as the rose tip opening.

3. Make the center bud, using tip 104. Hold nail containing base in your left (right) hand and bag with rose tip 104 in right (left) hand. Bag should be at a 45° angle to the flat surface of the nail and in the 4:30 (7:30) position.

4. Now you must do 3 things at the same time: squeeze the bag, move the tip and rotate the nail. As you squeeze the bag, move the tip up from the base, forming a ribbon of icing. Slowly turn the nail counterclockwise (clockwise for lefties) to bring the ribbon of icing around to overlap at the top of the mound, then back down to starting point. Move your tip straight up and down only; do not loop it around the base.

5. Now you have a finished center bud.

6. Make the top row of 3 petals. Touch the wide end of tip to the midpoint of bud base, narrow end straight up.

7. Turn nail, keeping wide end of tip on base so that petal will attach. Move tip up and back down to the midpoint of mound, forming the first petal. (Rotate the nail 1/3 turn for each petal.)

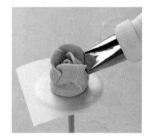

8. Start again, slightly behind end of first petal, and squeeze out second petal. Repeat for the third petal, ending by overlapping the starting point of the first petal.

9. Make the middle row of 5 petals. Touch the wide end of tip slightly below center of a petal in the top row. Angle the narrow end of tip out slightly more than you did for the top row of petals. Squeeze bag and turn nail moving tip up, then down, to form first petal.

10. Repeat for a total of 5 petals, rotating the nail 1/5 turn for each petal.

11. The last petal end should overlap the first's starting point.

12. Make the bottom row of 7 petals. Touch the wide end of tip below the center of a middle row petal, again angling the narrow end of tip out a little more. Squeeze bag and turn nail to end of fingers, moving tip up, then down to form first petal.

13. Repeat for a total of 7 petals, rotating the nail 1/7 turn for each petal.

14. The last petal end should overlap the first's starting point.

15. Slip waxed paper and completed rose from nail. This is the completed Wilton Rose.

Rosebud

Finish your petit fours or cupcakes with one pretty rosebud. Made in buttercream, this flat flower can be piped directly on the cake.

Practice With: Tips 104, 3

Icing Consistency: Stiff Consistency Buttercream for Petals, Thin Consistency for Sepals and Calyx

Bag Position: 45° at 4:30 (7:30) for petals; 45° at 6:00 for sepals and calyx

1. Using tip 104, make the base petal. Keep the narrow end of the tip raised up and slightly to the right (left for lefties). While squeezing, move the tip along the surface away from you in a straight line about 1/4 in. long. Pause, then continue squeezing as the icing fans out. Returning the tip to the original position and halfway back, start to release pressure, move tip to starting point,

stop pressure and pull tip away.

2. Using tip 104, make the overlapping petal. Touch the wide end of the tip to the outside edge of completed petal. The bag is positioned as for the base petal, at 4:30 (7:30); hold it steady in this position until the second petal is completed. As you continue squeezing, the icing will catch the edge of the base petal and roll over

it naturally. When the second petal looks complete, stop pressure completely, touch the tip back down to the surface and pull tip away.

3. Using tip 3, make the sepals and calyx. Form the middle sepal first by squeezing and letting icing build up. Lift the bag up and away from the flower. Stop pressure as you pull away to form the point of the sepal. Repeat, making

a sepal on the left and right sides. For the calyx, insert tip into the base of the center sepal. Squeeze, letting the icing build up. Slowly draw the tip toward you, relaxing pressure as you move away from the flower. Stop pressure, pull away. You may want to blend the calyx into the stem using a damp brush. Pipe tip 352 leaf, if desired.

Figure Piping

Figure piping is a way to really add personality to your cupcake. Figures can be as lifelike or cartoonish as you want them to be. Begin with a base, then add familiar shapes such as dots, balls and strings to give the figure personality. You may pipe directly on the cupcake using buttercream icing, or in advance on waxed paper using royal icing.

Clown

(see "Snack-In-The-Box", p. 9)

1. Pipe tip 32 mound for body.
2. Insert clown head. For arms, cut lollipop sticks to 2 3/4 in.; insert at

angle in cupcake, leaving 1 1/2 in. extended. Insert tip 32 over sticks; pull out tip as you squeeze bag to pipe arms.

3. Position fondant lid. Pipe tip 5 dot hands.

Valentine Bears

(see "Cubby Love", p. 55)

1. Pipe tip 2A upright cone for body. Pipe tip 12 pull-out legs and arms, ball feet.
2. Position fondant heart. Pipe tip 12 pull-out arms. Pipe tip 3 ball hands

with dot fingers. Pipe tip 2A ball head (pat smooth with fingertip dipped in cornstarch).

3. Pipe tip 3 dot ears and muzzle (pat smooth with finger dipped in cornstarch). Add tip 1 dot eyes and nose, outline mouth.

Swan Head and Wings

(see "Swimming Swans", p. 86)

1. Tape patterns to cake board; cover with waxed paper. Using royal icing and tip 12, pipe ball head with heavy pressure. Decrease pressure as you pipe outline neck. Add tip 3 pull-out beak. Let dry overnight.

2. Pipe tip 352 pull-out wings. Let dry overnight. Carefully remove head from waxed paper; turn over and overpipe back with tip 12 (pat seam to blend with fingertip dipped in cornstarch). Let dry overnight.

3. Draw dot eyes with black FoodWriter. Follow project instructions for piping body on cupcake; insert head and wings.

Other Decorating Techniques (cont.)

Fondant Twist Garland
(see "The Wishmaker", p. 4; "Group Wedding", p. 95)

1. Roll out fondant 1/16 in. thick. Using straight-edge wheel of Cutter/Embosser, cut 3/16 in. wide ribbon strips, about 2 in. long.

2. Twist the strips a few times.

3. Attach ends of strips with icing along edge of cupcake to form garland. Trim as needed.

Puddle Faces
(see "Smile Markers", p. 20; "Kids Take the Wheel!", p. 21; "Solo Flight", "Follow That Car", p. 28; "Hello, Copter", p. 29; "Luscious Loot", p. 30; "Enchanted Carriage", p. 39;)

Thin royal icing, adding 1/2 teaspoon water per 1/4 cup of icing. Icing is ready for flowing when a small amount dipped back into mixture takes a count of 10

to disappear. On waxed paper, pipe a ball, 3/4 to 1 1/4 in. diameter, depending on project instructions, using thinned royal icing in a cut parchment bag.

Let dry 48 hours. Decorate following project instructions.

Grill Legs & Connectors
(see "A Snack with Sizzle", p. 18)

For legs, cut cookie sticks into 3 in. lengths. Wrap sticks with foil; secure with glue. For leg connectors, shape 3 balls of red clay, 1/2 in. diameter. Turn cakes flat side down and attach balls with melted candy. Immediately insert legs at angle, 1/2 in. deep into cake. Turn cakes upright, making sure each is level. Turn back to flat side to set.

Pilot (see "Solo Flight", p. 28)
For pilot's body, cut large spice drop horizontally in half; attach top half to cone. For steering wheel, use gray wafer candy; attach with melted candy supporting against body with a piece of spice drop. For arms, roll out bottom spice drop half on waxed paper sprinkled with granulated sugar; cut strips and attach from body to steering wheel. Pipe tip 2 dot hands and fingers in buttercream. For face, use peach wafer candy; pipe tip 1 dot eyes and string mouth; add tip 2 pull-out hair. Attach to body, supporting with spice drop piece.

Dress, Girl, Cone Base and Crown
(see "Princess Takes a Dip", p. 39)

For dress, shape cereal treats mixture into half-ball shapes, 2 1/2 in. diameter x 2 in. high. Let cool on waxed paper. Place treats on cooling grid over cookie sheet; cover with melted pink candy. Refrigerate until firm; repeat for a 2nd coat if needed. Cut lollipop stick to 3 in.; insert into top center of treat. Tint a 2 in. ball of fondant rose and a 1 1/2 in. ball copper; add 1/4 teaspoon Gum-Tex to each. Reserve copper. For body, shape a 1 1/4 x 1 in. diameter log in rose. Insert on stick, leaving 3/4 in. extended at top for head. For arms, shape 3/4 x 1/2 in. diameter logs in rose; attach to body with damp brush. For hands, shape

3/8 in. balls in copper; make slits for fingers with knife. Attach with damp brush.

Roll out rose fondant 1/8 in. thick. Cut a 1/4 x 3 in. long strip for waistband; attach with damp brush. Reserve remaining rose fondant. For head, using reserved copper, shape a 1 1/8 in. ball; position on stick. For nose, shape a 1/8 in. copper ball; attach with damp brush. Draw eyes and mouth with FoodWriter. For cone base; place largest Cut-Out on cookie sheet; fill with melted white candy, 1/4 in. thick. Refrigerate until firm.

Using royal icing, pipe tip 2 swirl hair. Pipe tip 2 dot necklace; add tip 2 bead heart pendant. Pipe tip 3 double drop strings on dress; pipe tip 3 dot at string points. Pipe tip 2 small dots randomly on dress. For crown, tint small portions of fondant violet and dark rose. Roll out reserved rose fondant 1/8 in. thick (tint additional if needed). Trace crown pattern with toothpick; cut with knife. Roll in a circle; attach ends with damp brush. Roll small balls of violet and dark rose; attach with damp brush.

Other Decorating Techniques (cont.)

Purse Handles

(see "Purse-onal Treats", p. 40)

Tint portions of fondant violet, rose and yellow; add a small amount of Gum-Tex. For violet and yellow handles, roll a 7 x 1/4 in. diameter log. Using 3rd largest heart cutter as a guide, shape violet handle.

Shape yellow handle as shown.

For rose handle, roll an 8 1/2 x 1/4 in. diameter log; shape into a curve.

Eaves

(see "Home Tweet Home", p. 44)

1. Tape pattern to cake board; cover with waxed paper. Outline eaves with tip 2 and full-strength royal icing.

2. Flow in with thinned royal icing in cut disposable bag. Make extras to allow for breakage and let dry overnight.

3. Attach eaves to birdhouse cookies.

Candy Heart Shell

(see "Ripe for Romance", p. 56)

1. Place baking cups on cookie sheet. Fill with 2 tablespoons melted candy. Brush candy up sides, coating evenly to make heart candy shell. Refrigerate until firm.

2. Peel cup from candy, gently pushing up shell from bottom.

3. Keep shell in cool, dry place until ready to fill and serve.

Fondant Flowers

(see "Bonnet Season", p. 58; "Bridal Blossoms", "Carried When You're Married", p. 90; "Heart-Topped Tiers", p. 92)

1. Roll out fondant 1/8 in. thick. Cut flowers using Cut-Outs or cutters from Wilton Flower Making Sets.

2. Move flowers to thick shaping foam. Cup using ball tool from Confectionery Tool Set. Let dry in Flower Formers dusted with cornstarch.

3. Add flower centers in icing following project instructions.

Candy Faces

(see "The Vampire Retires", p. 65)

Make faces in the Candy Melting Plate; fill cavities with melted Candy Melts® using a cut decorating bag. Refrigerate until firm and unmold.

Place faces on waxed paper-covered board and decorate facial features using melted candy in cut bag.

Candy Shell Hood
(see "Baby's Bassinette", p. 72)

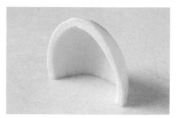

1. Fill Mini Egg Pan cavities to top edge with melted candy. Tap on counter to remove air bubbles. Let chill in refrigerator for 10-15 minutes or until a 1/4 in. shell has formed. Pour out excess candy; smooth top

edges with spatula and chill for 15-20 minutes longer.

2. Carefully unmold shells (if you have difficulty removing shells, place in freezer for 2-3 minutes, then

unmold). With knife, cut off lower 1/3 of shell; smooth cut edge with finger.

3. Position top 2/3 of shell on cupcake for hood.

Fondant Rope
(see "Fruit Basket", p. 78; "Bridal Blossoms", p. 90)

1. Roll fondant into logs using palms of hands (see cake instructions for specific dimensions). You will need 2 pieces of the same length. Lay the pieces side by side and gently press together at one end to join.

2. Holding the joined end in a stationary position, twist the other end 2 or 3 complete turns. Continue twisting as needed.

3. Attach rope to cupcake using a damp brush.

Fondant Bow Loops
(see "Bold Bows", p. 89)

1. Roll out fondant 1/8 in. thick. Cut strips using dimensions listed in project instructions.

2. Fold strips in half, brush ends with water and press together to form loops. Let dry on sides on cornstarch-dusted cake board.

3. Insert loops in cupcake, securing with icing if needed.

Flower Cascades
(see Festive Florals, p. 91)

Base Bouquet (Make 13): Gather 7 large and 5 small flowers together, tape together 1 1/4 in. below flower calyxes.

Spray (Make 8): Begin with 1 large flower. Tape a 2nd large flower with a 1 in. stem 1 1/2 in. below calyx of first flower. Measure 1 in. below that point and attach 1 large and 1 small flower with 1 in. stems. Measure 1 in. and attach 3 large flowers with 1 in. stems. Bend the spray at this point.

Side Spray (Make 4): Begin with 1 large flower. Measure 2 in. below calyx and attach a group of 3 large and 3 small flowers, all with 1 in. stems. Bend the spray at this point.

1. Make 1 floral cascade for the top consisting of a base bouquet and 4 side sprays.

2. Make 4 floral bouquets for the middle level consisting of only the base bouquet.

3. Make 8 floral cascades for the bottom level consisting of a base bouquet and a spray.

Ribbon Roses
(see "Romance Arose", p. 92)

Roll out fondant 1/16 in. thick. Cut a 1 x 6 in. rectangle. Begin rolling from one end of strip, gradually loosening strip as flower gets larger. Open petals between spirals using veining tool.

Patterns

Multiple patterns used for the same project are shaded in the same color. For left and right side decorations, like hands, reverse the pattern if only one appears.

Hat

Hand

Hand

Hand

Hand

Hands (see "A Clown's Never Down," p. 11)

Hands and Hat
(see "Stand Up and Cheer," p. 4;
Instructions, p. 96)

Legs
(see "Up in Arms," p. 24;
"Cupcake Crawler," p. 66)

Hand

Hand
(see "Silly Feet Treats," p. 11)

Top Fin, Side Fin, and Tail
(see "School's in Session," p. 25)

Water Spout
(see "Moby Quick," p. 24)

Hand

Hand
(see "Screamin' Demons," p. 33)

Top Fin

Side Fin

Tail

Facemask
(see "Grab the
Facemask," p. 34)

Soccer Ball
Panel

Taco (see "Taco Supreme," p. 18)

Soccer Ball
Panel

Bow Tie

Eye

Soccer Ball
(see "Just Kickin' Back," p. 34)

Cheek

Button

Hand

Shoe

Mouth

Hat

Hair

Hat, Hand, Eye, Cheek, Button, Hair, Shoe, Bow
Tie, and Mouth (see "Jolly Juggler," p. 27)

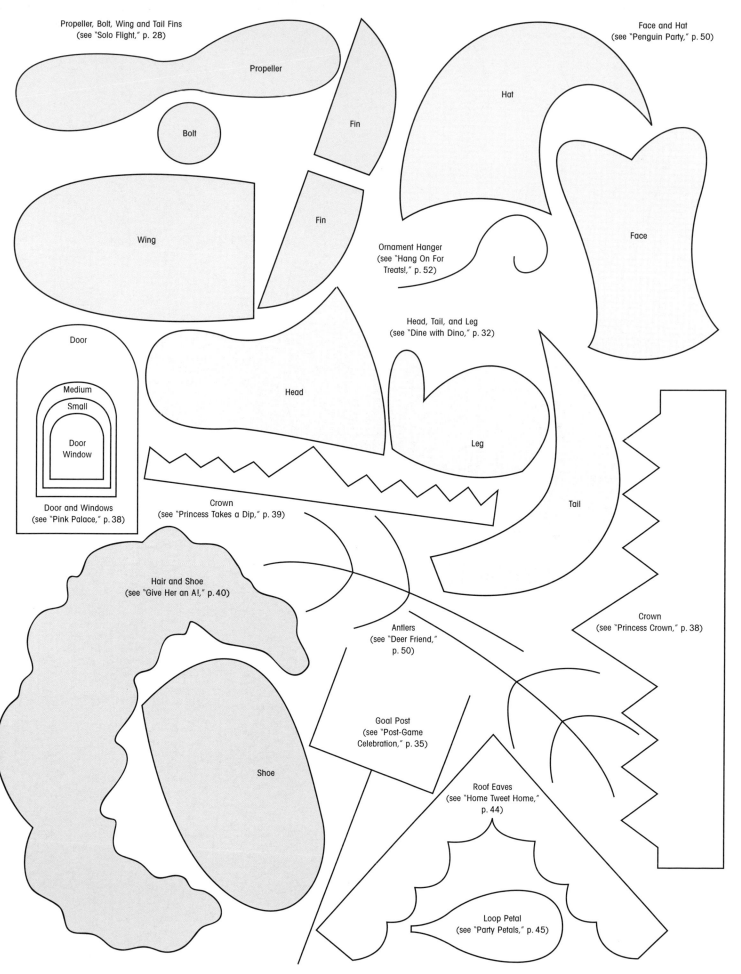

Propeller, Bolt, Wing and Tail Fins
(see "Solo Flight," p. 28)

Propeller

Bolt

Fin

Fin

Wing

Face and Hat
(see "Penguin Party," p. 50)

Hat

Face

Ornament Hanger
(see "Hang On For Treats!," p. 52)

Head, Tail, and Leg
(see "Dine with Dino," p. 32)

Head

Leg

Tail

Door

Medium

Small

Door Window

Door and Windows
(see "Pink Palace," p. 38)

Crown
(see "Princess Takes a Dip," p. 39)

Crown
(see "Princess Crown," p. 38)

Hair and Shoe
(see "Give Her an A!," p. 40)

Antlers
(see "Deer Friend," p. 50)

Goal Post
(see "Post-Game Celebration," p. 35)

Shoe

Roof Eaves
(see "Home Tweet Home," p. 44)

Loop Petal
(see "Party Petals," p. 45)

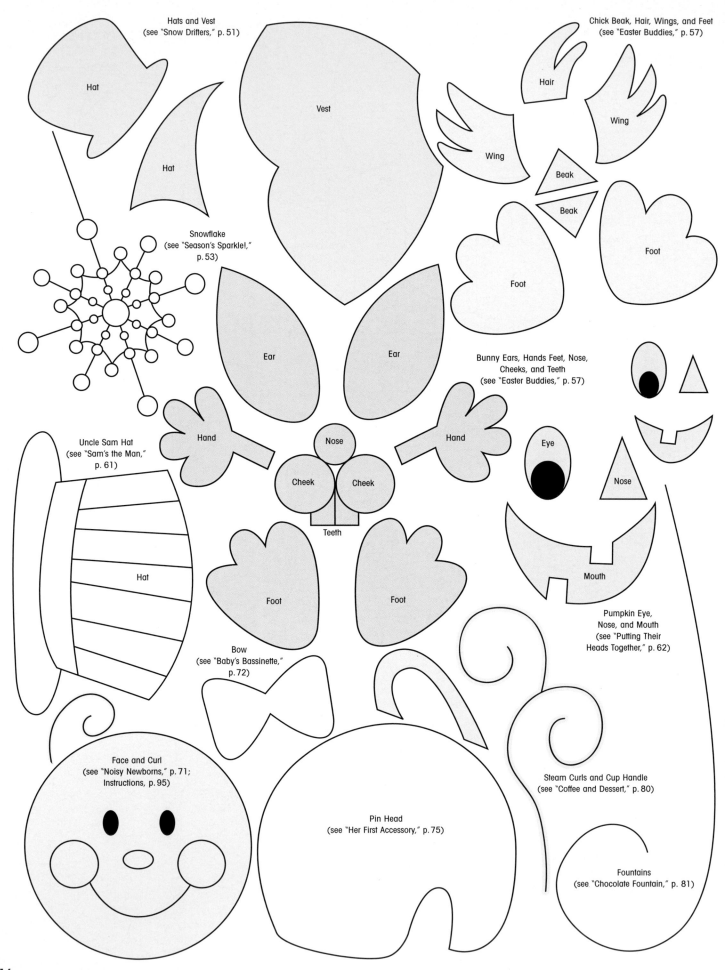

Hats and Vest
(see "Snow Drifters," p. 51)

Hat

Hat

Vest

Chick Beak, Hair, Wings, and Feet
(see "Easter Buddies," p. 57)

Hair

Wing

Wing

Beak

Beak

Foot

Foot

Snowflake
(see "Season's Sparkle!,"
p. 53)

Ear

Ear

Bunny Ears, Hands Feet, Nose,
Cheeks, and Teeth
(see "Easter Buddies," p. 57)

Uncle Sam Hat
(see "Sam's the Man,"
p. 61)

Hand

Nose

Hand

Eye

Cheek

Cheek

Eye

Nose

Teeth

Hat

Foot

Foot

Mouth

Pumpkin Eye,
Nose, and Mouth
(see "Putting Their
Heads Together," p. 62)

Bow
(see "Baby's Bassinette,"
p. 72)

Face and Curl
(see "Noisy Newborns," p. 71;
Instructions, p. 95)

Pin Head
(see "Her First Accessory," p. 75)

Steam Curls and Cup Handle
(see "Coffee and Dessert," p. 80)

Fountains
(see "Chocolate Fountain," p. 81)

Bodice
(see "Here's to a Happy Beginning," p. 88)

Bow
(see "A Romantic Ring,"
p. 86)

Easel
(see "Here's to a
Happy Beginning," p. 88)

Veil
(see "Here's to a
Happy Beginning," p. 88)

Wing

Chocolate Swirls
(see "Ganache Grandeur," p. 81)

Tuxedo Jacket, Shirt,
Lapels, Pants, Shoes
(see "Here's to a Happy Beginning," p. 88)

Head

Shirt/Lapels and Bow Tie
(see "Formal Fare," p. 93)

Tuxedo
Jacket

Head and Wings
(see "Swimming Swans," p. 86)

Bow Tie

Wing

Lapel

Shirt

Lapel

Shirt

Lapel

Lapel

Veil
(see "Group Wedding," p. 83;
Instructions, p. 95)

Pants

Shoe

Shoe

Cupcake Products

What makes Wilton cupcakes more fun? It's our exciting products, which make baking, decorating and serving one-of-a-kind cupcakes a pleasure! In this section, you'll find just about everything you need to create the terrific designs featured in this book. For a complete selection of decorating tips, tools, toppers, seasonal baking cups and more, see your Wilton retailer, visit our website at www.wilton.com or check the latest edition of the Wilton Yearbook of Cake Decorating. Remember to check back often for exciting new products—our selection changes regularly and some products listed may no longer be available.

Jumbo Sprinkles

Give your cupcakes a big finish! Top them with our new Jumbo Sprinkles in exciting shapes and colors. These big and bold decorations are perfect for cupcakes, mini cakes, jumbo and king-size cupcakes, brownies and cookies.

Innovative shapes for birthday, holiday and wedding designs. 2.8 oz. bottles unless otherwise noted. Certified Kosher.

Jumbo Daisies
710-028

Jumbo Hearts
710-032

Jumbo Confetti
710-029

Jumbo Stars
710-026

Jumbo Diamonds
710-027

Jumbo Rainbow Nonpareils
4.8 oz. bottle
710-033

Shaped Sprinkles

Pour on the fun! Great shapes and colors add a dash of excitement to cakes, cupcakes, ice cream and more. Certified Kosher.

Sour Cherry Balls
4.4 oz. bottle
710-034

Heart Drops
5.25 oz. bottle
710-035

White Nonpareils
3 oz. bottle
710-773

Rainbow Jimmies
2.5 oz. bottle
710-776

Rainbow Nonpareils
3 oz. bottle
710-772

Valentine Nonpareils
3 oz. bottle
710-625

Patriotic Mix
2.5 oz. bottle
710-786

Autumn Leaves
2.5 oz. bottle
710-787

Hallow Pumpkin Mix
2.5 oz. bottle
710-182

Halloween Nonpareils
3 oz. bottle
710-584

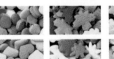
Flowerful Medley
Includes Confetti, Colorful Leaves, Daisies, Pastel Hearts, Wild Flowers, Butterflies. 2.23 oz. bottle
710-4122

Sparkling Sugars

Put that extra dazzle in your decorating! These easy-pour sugars have a coarse texture and a brilliant sparkle that makes cupcakes, cookies and cakes really shine. 8 oz. bottle. Certified Kosher.

Pink
710-038

Lavender
710-037

Yellow
710-036

Blue
710-039

Colored Sugars

Extra-fine sugar is excellent for filling in brightly colored designs on cakes, cupcakes and cookies. 3.25 oz. bottle. Certified Kosher.

Blue
710-750

Light Green
710-752

Orange
710-759

Red
710-766

Dark Green
710-764

Black
710-762

Icing Decorations
Certified Kosher.

Graduation
710-1125 Pk./12

Flag
710-726 Pk./9

Football
710-478 Pk./9

Petite Ghosts
710-3030 Pk./12

Icings

All Wilton icings are formulated for decorating as well as taste. That's because Wilton insists on providing you with the perfect consistency icing for decorating. Our quality ingredients mean better results for you.

Ready-To-Use Decorator Icings

Wilton makes the only ready-to-use icing that is the perfect consistency for decorating. The pure white color is best for creating true vivid colors using Wilton Icing Colors. Rich and creamy, with a delicious homemade taste. Certified Kosher.

1 lb. Can

Ideal stiff consistency for making roses and flowers with upright petals. One 16 oz. can covers two 8 or 9 in. layers or one 9 x 13 in. cake.

White 710-118 Certified Kosher Dairy.
Chocolate 710-119

Vanilla Whipped Icing Mix

Our light, whipped icing is the ideal texture for decorating in an easy-to-make, delicious mix. Just add ice water and it whips up velvety-smooth for icing or decorating. Light and delicate flavor. Each 10 oz. box makes 4 cups. Certified Kosher Dairy.

710-1241

White Ready-To-Use Rolled Fondant

Fondant has never been more convenient and easy for decorating! With Wilton Ready-To-Use Rolled Fondant, there's no mess, no guesswork. The 24 oz. (1½ lbs.) package covers an 8 in. 2-layer cake plus decorations; the 80 oz. (5 lbs.) package covers a 2-layer 6 in., 8 in. and 10 in. round tiered cake plus decorations. Pure white. Certified Kosher.

24 oz. (1½ lbs.) Pk. 710-2076
80 oz. (5 lbs.) Pk. 710-2180

Color Fondant Multi Packs

Convenient four-pouch assortments of primary, neon, pastel or natural colors are perfect for making multi-colored decorations. The color is already mixed in... no kneading, no mess, no guesswork. Great for flowers, borders and fun shapes. Each 17.6 oz. package contains four 4.4 oz. packs. Certified Kosher.

Primary Colors	Neon Colors	Pastel Colors	Natural Colors
Green, Red, Yellow, Blue	Purple, Orange, Yellow, Pink	Blue, Yellow, Pink, Green	Light Brown, Dark Brown, Pink, Black
710-445	**710-446**	**710-447**	**710-448**

Meringue Powder

Primary ingredient for royal icing. Stabilizes buttercream, adds body to boiled icing and meringue. Replaces egg whites in many recipes. Resealable top opens for easy measuring. 4 oz. can makes 5 recipes of royal icing; 8 oz. can makes 10 recipes. 16 oz. can makes 20 recipes. Certified Kosher.

4 oz. can 702-6007
8 oz. can 702-6015
16 oz. can 702-6004

Piping Gel

Pipe messages and designs or glaze cakes before icing. Use clear or tint with icing color. 10 oz. Certified Kosher.

704-105

Clear Vanilla Extract
2 fl. oz. **604-2237**

Color Flow Mix

Create dimensional flow-in designs for your cake. Just add water and confectioners' sugar. 4 oz. can makes ten 1½ cup batches. Certified Kosher.

701-47

Gum-Tex™

Makes fondant and gum paste pliable, elastic, easy to shape. Plastic resealable lid. 6 oz.

707-117

Bake Easy!™ Non-Stick Spray

For cakes that turn out beautifully every time, start by spraying pans with Bake Easy. This convenient non-stick spray helps your cakes release perfectly with fewer crumbs for easier icing and a flawless look for decorating. Just a light, even coating does the job. Use Bake Easy for all mixes and recipes—cupcakes, brownies, breads and more. Versatile for all types of baking and cooking. 6 oz.

702-6018

Cake Release

No need to grease and flour your baking pan—Cake Release coats in one step. Simply spread Cake Release lightly on pan bottom and sides with a pastry brush and add batter. Cakes release perfectly without crumbs every time, giving you the ideal surface for decorating. In convenient dispensing bottle. 8 fl. oz. Certified Kosher.

702-6016

Icing Colors

Wilton color is made to produce deeper, richer color by adding just a small amount. Our concentrated gel formula helps you achieve the exact shade you want without thinning your icing. You'll find a rainbow of colors, ready to blend together for creating your own custom shades.

Primary 4-Icing Colors Set

Lemon Yellow, Sky Blue, Christmas Red, Brown in .5 oz. jars. Certified Kosher.

601-5127 Set/4

8-Icing Colors Set

Lemon Yellow, Sky Blue, Christmas Red, Brown, Orange, Violet, Pink and Leaf Green in .5 oz. jars. Certified Kosher.

601-5577 Set/8

12-Icing Colors Set

Our most popular collection creates the spectrum of primary colors plus skin tones, teal and burgundy. Teal, Brown, Violet, Burgundy, Royal Blue, Kelly Green, Lemon Yellow, No-Taste Red, Copper (skin tone), Pink, Golden Yellow, Black in .5 oz. jars. Certified Kosher. **601-5580 Set/12**

Pastel 4-Icing Colors Set

Willow Green, Cornflower Blue, Creamy Peach, Rose Petal Pink in .5 oz. jars. Certified Kosher.

601-25588 Set/4

Garden Tone 4-Icing Colors Set

Buttercup Yellow, Delphinium Blue, Aster Mauve, Juniper Green in .5 oz. jars. Certified Kosher.

601-4240 Set/4

FoodWriter™ Edible Color Markers

Use like ink markers to add fun and dazzling color to countless foods. Kids love 'em! Decorate on fondant, color flow, royal icing, even directly on cookies. Brighten everyday foods like toaster pastries, cheese, fruit slices, bread and more. Each set includes five .35 oz. FoodWriter pens. Certified Kosher.

Primary Colors Sets

Yellow	Green	Red	Blue	Black

Fine Tip 609-100 Set/5   **Bold Tip 609-115 Set/5**

Neon Colors Set

Purple	Orange	Pink	Light Green	Black

Fine Tip 609-116 Set/5

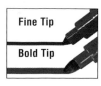

Fine Tip

Bold Tip

Color Accents
Color Mist™ Food Color Spray

This easy-to-use spray gives decorators the versatility and dazzling effects of an airbrush in a convenient can! Creates a rainbow of excitement on so many desserts. Use it to transform a plain iced cake with sensational color, add splashes of holiday color to iced cookies and cupcakes. Great for party desserts—highlighting whipped topping or ice cream with color. No mess, taste-free formula; add a little color or a lot. 1.5 oz. Certified Kosher.

Red 710-5500
Blue 710-5501
Yellow 710-5502
Green 710-5503
Violet 710-5504
Pink 710-5505

Cake Sparkles

Add shimmering color to cakes, cupcakes, cookies and ice cream! Brilliant edible glitter in a great variety of colors, great for stencilling, highlighting messages, snow scenes. .25 oz. Certified Kosher.

White 703-1290
Red 703-1284
Blue 703-1314

Shimmer Dust™

Give your fondant decorating that added dash of color—sprinkle on Shimmer Dust! Just brush your fondant-covered cake top or fondant Cut-Outs with water and sprinkle lightly over the dampened area. Total net wt. .47 oz. Certified Kosher.

Elegant Colors: Silver, Gold, Pearl 703-212 **Set/3**

Silicone Baking Cups

Discover the convenience and easy release of flexible silicone! Reusable oven-safe cups in fun colors and exciting shapes are perfect for baking and serving.

Silly-Feet! Silicone Baking Cups
Orange, Yellow, Blue, Purple. Cups are 2 in. diameter. 2⁵/₁₆ in. high with feet.
415-9428 Pk./4

    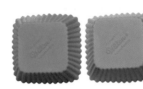 

Diamond Baking Cups
6 Yellow, 6 Red. 3 in. wide.
415-9419 Pk./12

Triangle Baking Cups
6 Pink, 6 Purple. 2³/₈ in. wide.
415-9423 Pk./12

Square Baking Cups
6 Blue, 6 Green. 2 in. wide.
415-9424 Pk./12

Heart Baking Cups
6 Pink, 6 Red. 2 in. wide.
415-9409 Pk./12

Halloween Baking Cups
6 Orange, 6 Purple. Standard size, 2 in. diameter.
415-9408 Pk./12

Pastel Baking Cups
3 Yellow, 3 Green, 3 Pink, 3 Blue. Standard size, 2 in. diameter.
415-9410 Pk./12

Christmas Baking Cups
6 Green, 6 Red. Standard size, 2 in. diameter.
415-9405 Pk./12

Baking Cups

A quick, easy and fun way to dress up a cupcake! Great for holding candy, nuts and party snacks! Made of microwave-safe paper in novel prints, stripes and solids. King-size and jumbo cups are 2¼ in. diameter, standard cups are 2 in. diameter, mini cups are 1¼ in. diameter.

Cupcake Heaven
Standard 415-422 **Pk./75**
Mini 415-426 **Pk./100**

White
King-Size 415-2118 **Pk./24**
Jumbo 415-2503 **Pk/50**
Standard 415-2505 **Pk./75**
Mini 415-2507 **Pk./100**

Pastel Baking Cups
Standard
25 pink, 25 yellow, 25 blue.
415-394 **Pk./75**

Gold Foil Baking Cups
Wax-laminated paper on foil.
Standard 415-206 **Pk./24**
Bon Bon 415-306 **Pk./75**

Silver Foil Baking Cups
Standard 415-207
24 pure aluminum/24 paper
Bon Bon 415-307
36 pure aluminum/36 paper

Foil Petite Loaf Cups*
Wax-laminated paper on foil.
Gold Foil 415-452 **Pk./24**
White Foil 415-450 **Pk./24**
*Petite Loaf Cups are 3³/₄ x 1¹/₂ in. and fit Petite Loaf Pan p. 122.

Baking Cups

Patriotic Stars
Standard 415-2235 Pk./75

Stripes
Standard 415-5381 Pk./75
Mini 415-5380 Pk./100

Bunnies & Chicks
Standard 415-515 Pk./75
Mini 415-547 Pk./100

Autumn Leaves
Standard 415-431 Pk./75
Mini 415-433 Pk./100

Spooky Ghosts
Standard 415-1601 Pk./75
Mini 415-2027 Pk./100

Smiling Pumpkin
Standard 415-324 Pk./75
Mini 415-7572 Pk./100

Soccer
Standard 415-296 Pk./50

Football
Standard 415-297 Pk./50

Smiley Grad
Standard 415-4592 Pk./75

Graduation
Standard 415-4594 Pk./75

Old Glory
Standard 415-2236 Pk./75

Non-Stick Bakeware

Our premium non-stick bakeware combines superior non-stick performance, serving convenience and elegant design, to provide the highest level of baking satisfaction.

Mini Tasty-Fill™ Cake Pan Set

Create filled single-serving desserts with incredible flavor combinations using these convenient non-stick pans. The patented recessed design forms a contour you can fill with ice cream, fruit, mousse and more. A delicious surprise in every bite. Set includes four 4 x 1¼ in. non-stick pans; bonus recipe book with delicious ideas and complete instructions.

2105-155 Set/4

6-Cup King-Size Muffin Pan

Create extra-tall treats that make an impact at any celebration! Great for cupcakes, mini angel food cakes, molded gelatin, ice cream and mousse. Heavy-gauge premium non-stick for quick release and easy clean-up.

2105-9921

24 Cup Mini Muffin Pan
2105-914

12 Cup Muffin Pan
2105-954

6 Cup Muffin Pan
2105-953

Jumbo Muffin Pan
2105-955

Mini Loaf Pan
2105-949 5¾ x 9 x 2⅛ in.

8 in. Square Pan
2105-956 8 x 8 x 2 in.

Oblong Cake Pan
2105-961 9 x 13 x 2 in.

2105-968
Jelly Roll Pans
2105-966 Small 13¼ x 9¼ x ⅝ in.
2105-967 Medium 15¼ x 10¼ x ¾ in.
2105-968 Large 17¼ x 11½ x 1 in.

Jumbo Cookie Sheet
2105-978 18 x 14 in.

Large Cookie Sheet
2105-977 16 x 14 in.

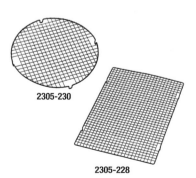

2305-230

2305-228

Cooling Grids
10 x 16 in. Rectangle
2305-228
14½ x 20 in. Rectangle
2305-229
13 in. Round
2305-230

Aluminum Bakeware

Better bakeware means better baking results—that's why bakers and decorators have counted on Wilton for generations. Wilton aluminum bakeware is built to be the most durable and even heating—our pans will hold their shape through years of use. The Wilton selection is also unmatched. Whether you're baking cupcakes or a tiered wedding cake, we have the quality bakeware you need.

Jumbo Muffin Pan
Make super-size cupcakes and muffins. Six cups, each 4 x 2 in.
2105-1820

Petite Loaf Pan
Great for single-size dessert cakes, frozen bread dough. Nine cavities, each 2¹/₂ x 3³/₈ x 1¹/₂ in.
2105-8466

Mini Loaf Pans
Everyone loves personal-sized nut breads or cakes. Six cavities are 4¹/₂ x 2¹/₂ x 1¹/₂ in.
2105-9791

Mini Ball Pan
Ice two mini balls and push together for a 3-D effect. One cake mix makes 10-12 mini balls. Six cavities, each 3¹/₂ x 3¹/₂ x 1¹/₂ in. deep.
2105-1760

Standard Muffin Pan
Most popular size for morning muffins, after-school cupcakes and desserts. Twelve cups, each 3 in. diameter x 1 in.
2105-9310

Mini Egg Pan
Make colorful place markers for the holiday table. One mix makes about 24-36 eggs. 8 cavities, each 3¹/₄ x 2¹/₂ x 1 in. deep.
2105-2118

Square Pan
8 x 2 in.
2105-8191

Jelly Roll and Cookie Pans
Wilton pans are 1 in. deep for fuller-looking desserts.

10¹/₂ x 15¹/₂ x 1 in.
2105-1269
12 x 18 x 1 in.
2105-4854

2105-1269

Sheet Pan
9 x 13 x 2 in.
2105-1308

Cookie Sheet
Extra-thick construction heats evenly for perfectly browned bottoms.

Jumbo 14 x 20 in.
2105-6213
12¹/₂ x 16¹/₂ in.
2105-2975

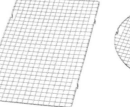

Insulated Cookie Sheet
Two quality aluminum layers sandwich an insulating layer of air for perfect browning without burning.

14 x 16 in.
2105-2644

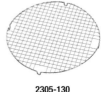

Cooling Grids
10 x 16 in. Rectangle
2305-128
14¹/₂ x 20 in. Rectangle
2305-129
13 in. Round
2305-130

2305-129

2305-130

Cupcake Carriers

Cupcake Boxes
Brightly-patterned window boxes are the perfect way to hold and display your cupcakes! Each box includes an insert with recessed space to hold standard cupcakes safely in place. Easy folding assembly; great for gifts and favors! Choose single or 4-cupcake size.

Cupcake Heaven
Holds 1 standard cupcake.
415-289 Pk./3
Holds 4 standard cupcakes.
415-1206 Pk./3

415-289

415-1206

Snappy Stripes
Holds 1 standard cupcake.
415-1205 Pk./3
Holds 4 standard cupcakes.
415-948 Pk./3

415-1205

415-948

The Ultimate 3-In-1 Caddy™
It's the most convenient way to take along cakes, cupcakes, muffins and more! The Ultimate 3-In-1 Caddy features an exclusive reversible cupcake tray which holds 12 standard or 24 mini cupcakes. Or, remove the tray to carry up to a 9 x 13 in. decorated cake on the sturdy locking base. The see-through cover has higher sides to protect icing flowers and tall decorations. You can also use the caddy at home, to keep pies, cookies and brownies fresh for days after baking.
17.9 x 14.4 x 6.8 in. high.
2105-9958

Cupcake Displays

Cupcakes 'N More® Dessert Stands

Individually decorated cupcakes are the perfect way to add a personal touch to celebrations. Now, with Cupcakes 'N More, you have the perfect way to serve them! The look is fresh and fun, featuring bold silver-finished wire spirals to securely hold each cupcake. The twisting, towering design is perfect for any setting—showers, kids' birthdays, weddings, holidays and more.

Easy to assemble!
Just stack each layer of cupcakes onto the locking center rod.

Keeps looking great!
Non-toxic, silver-finished metal has a durable non-chip finish.

Collapsible design
Stores easily and safely.

Angled holders
Give the best view of cupcake tops!

13 Count Dessert Stand
9¼ in. high x 9 in. wide.
Holds 13 standard cupcakes.
307-831

19 Count Party Stand
18 in. high x 12 in. wide.
Holds 19 standard cupcakes.
307-666

38 Count Dessert Stand
15 in. high x 18 wide.
Holds 38 standard cupcakes.
307-651

23 Count Dessert Stand
12 in. high x 13 wide.
Holds 23 standard cupcakes.
307-826

24 Count Mini Dessert Stand
10½ in. high x 9 in. wide.
Holds 24 mini cupcakes.
307-250

Cupcake Pedestals

Give your cupcakes a lift and show off your desserts with these fun plastic display pedestals! Easy to assemble—twist the top platform onto the stem base. Cupcake Pedestals perfectly display cupcakes, muffins, party favors and more— or turn the pedestal over for the perfect ice cream cone holder!

307-839 Pk./4

Silly Feet Cake and Treat Stand

Everyone will get a kick out of your cake when it's served on this fun, footed stand. Just insert the plate onto the foot support, add your decorated cake, cupcakes or other desserts and watch your friends make tracks to your treats. Take the fun a step further by surrounding the stand with cupcakes baked in our Silly-Feet! Silicone Baking Cups. Includes 10 in. plate which holds an 8 or 9 in. round cake and foot support piece.

307-878

Cookie Cutters
101 Cookie Cutters!
With this set, you're covered! Make cookies featuring popular holiday and theme shapes like sports, flowers, animals and more. Or use the complete alphabet and numeral collections included to create the perfect cookie message. Great for cutting all kinds of food into fun shapes—perfect for crafting, too. Average cutter size approx. 3$\frac{1}{2}$ x 3$\frac{1}{2}$ in. Recipe included.

2304-1000 Set/101

A-B-C and 1-2-3 50-Pc. Cutter Set
Complete alphabet and numeral collection, great for cookies, brownies, gelatin treats, learning games, crafts and more. Average cutter size approx. 3$\frac{1}{2}$ x 3$\frac{1}{2}$ in. Recipe included.

2304-1054 Set/50

Animal Pals 50-Pc. Cutter Set
Everyone will go wild for cookies, foods and crafts made with this menagerie of favorite animal shapes. Shapes include fish, dog, cat, birds, butterflies, reptiles and more. Average cutter size approx. 3$\frac{1}{2}$ x 3$\frac{1}{2}$ in. Recipe included.

2304-1055 Set/50

Hearts Nesting Cutter Set
Sizes from 1$\frac{1}{2}$ to 4$\frac{1}{8}$ in.

2304-115 Set/6

Bunnies Nesting Cutter Set
Sizes from 1$\frac{1}{4}$ to 4$\frac{1}{8}$ in.

2303-9270 Set/4

Metal Cookie Cutters

Gingerbread Boys Nesting Cutter Set
Largest is approx. 5 in.
2308-1239 Set/4

Gingerbread Boy
Approx. 3 in.
2308-1002

Circle
3 in. diameter.
2308-1010

Blossoms Nesting Set
Pretty flowers in four sizes. Largest is approx. 5 in.
2308-1204 Set/4

Valentine Cutter Collection
Vivid Valentine colors bring a touch of romance to cookie-baking. Great variety of hearts, hugs and kisses designs. Sizes range from 1 to 5 in. Colored aluminum.

2308-2502 Set/9

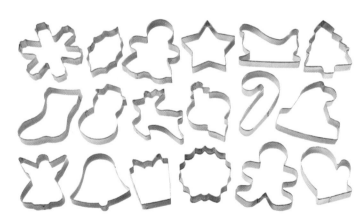

Holiday Cutter Set
Set of 18 includes snowflake, holly leaf, gingerbread girl, star, sleigh, tree, stocking, snowman, reindeer, ornament, candy cane, Santa hat, angel, bell, gift, wreath, gingerbread boy and mitten, each approx. 3 in.

2308-1132 Set/18

Leaves and Acorns Nesting Metal Cutter Set
Set of 9 includes graduated acorns, oak and maple leaves, (3 each). 1$\frac{3}{4}$ to 3$\frac{3}{4}$ in. Recipe included.

2308-2000 Set/9

Pumpkins Nesting Cutter Set
Create boo-tiful Halloween treats in four sizes. Each cuts neatly and is easy to handle. Sizes from 2$\frac{1}{4}$ to 4$\frac{1}{2}$ in. Recipe included.

2308-1210 Set/4

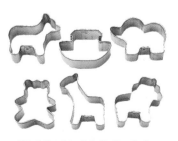

Mini Noah's Ark Cutter Set
Set of 6 includes horse, ark, elephant, bear, giraffe and lion. Each approx. 1$\frac{1}{2}$ in.

2308-1206 Set/6

Mini Romantic Cutter Set
Set of 6 includes butterfly, heart, bell, crinkled heart, tulip, and blossom. Each approx. 1$\frac{1}{2}$ in.

2308-1225 Set/6

Metal Cookie Cutters

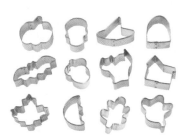

Holiday Mini Cutter Set
Set of 12 includes star, angel, gingerbread girl, stocking, candy cane, ornament, teddy bear, bell, holly leaf, tree, gingerbread boy and sleigh, each approx. 1½ in.
2308-1250 Set/12

Harvest Mini Cutter Set
Set of 6 includes oak leaf, maple leaf, apple, pumpkin, elm leaf and acorn, each approx. 1½ in.
2308-1217 Set/6

Halloween Mini Cutter Set
Set of 12 includes pumpkin, skull, witch's hat, tombstone, bat, acorn, cat, house, maple leaf, moon, oak leaf and ghost, each approx. 1½ in.
2308-1246 Set/12

Cut-Outs™ for Fondant

With Cut-Outs, it's easy to make fun 3-D shapes for your fondant cakes and cupcakes. Just roll out fondant, press down with Cut-Out and lift away. Remove shapes with a small spatula. Stainless steel shapes range from ⅝ in. to 2½ in.

Alphabet/Number	Heart	Leaf	Flower	Oval	Round	Square
417-442 Set/37	**417-434 Set/3**	**417-437 Set/3**	**417-435 Set/3**	**417-438 Set/3**	**417-432 Set/3**	**417-431 Set/3**

Decorating Tools

Cupcake Decorating Set
Make cupcakes exciting and fun with 4 versatile tips. Get ready to create novel designs for everyday treats using Star Tips 1M and 22, Round Tip 12 and Bismarck Tip 230. Set also includes: 8 disposable decorating bags and instruction booklet.
2104-6667 Set/13

9 in. Rolling Pin
Roll out fondant evenly, in the perfect thickness for easy cutting and shaping, with this 3-piece non-stick roller. Roll to the perfect ⅛ in. height used for cutting many fondant decorations, using the slide-on guide rings. Easy to handle—just the right size for preparing small amounts of fondant to place on your cake. Perfect for use with Fondant Multi Packs and Cut-Outs™. Pin is 9 x 1 in. diameter.
1907-1205

Cake Dividing Set
Measures equal sections of your cake for precise placement of garlands, stringwork and other designs. Cake Dividing Wheel marks up to 16 divisions on cakes up to 20 in. diameter. Garland Marker adjusts to 7 widths. Instructions included.
409-806 Set/2

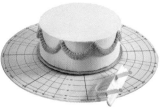

Brush Set
Add a special touch of color to your fondant-covered cake! It's easy and fun with these fine-bristle brushes. Three tip designs—round, square and bevel— help you achieve different painted effects using icing color or thinned icing. Also great for applying water or adhesive to attach fondant decorations.
1907-1207 Set/3

Flower Nail No. 7
For basic flower making. Provides the control you need when piping icing flowers. Just rotate the nail between your thumb and fingers as you pipe a flower on the head. Stainless steel. 1½ in.
402-3007

Floral Collection Flower Making Set
Make incredibly lifelike gum paste flowers. Full-color how-to book includes many arranging ideas and step-by-step instructions. Kit includes 24 plastic cutters, 1 leaf mold, 3 wood modeling tools, protector flap, 40-page instruction book and 2 foam squares for modeling.
1907-117 Set/32
Book only 907-117

Cookie Treat Sticks
For fun cookie pops.
6 in. 1912-9319 Pk./20
8 in. 1912-9318 Pk./20

Plastic Dowel Rods
Heavy-duty hollow plastic provides strong, sanitary support for all tiered cakes. Cut with serrated knife to desired length. Length: 12¾ in. diameter: ¾ in.
399-801 Pk./4

Non-Stick Parchment Paper
Use Wilton silicone-treated non-stick parchment to line baking pans and cookie sheets—a non-fat alternative that saves cleanup time. Roll out cookie dough between 2 sheets, dough won't stick and will easily transfer to your cookie sheet. You can even reuse it for the next batch. Oven-safe to 400°F. Parchment is great for conventional ovens, microwaves and the freezer. Double roll is 41 square feet, 15 in. wide. Certified Kosher.
415-680

Fanci-Foil
Serving side has a non-toxic grease-resistant surface. FDA-approved for use with food. Continuous roll: 20 in. x 15 ft.
Silver 804-167

Featherweight® Decorating Bags

Use these easy-handling bags over and over. Lightweight, strong and flexible polyester will never get stiff. Coated to prevent grease from seeping through. May be boiled; dishwasher safe. Instructions included. Sold singly.

8 in. 404-5087
10 in. 404-5109
12 in. 404-5125
14 in. 404-5140
16 in. 404-5168
18 in. 404-5184

Disposable Decorating Bags

Just use, then toss. Strong, flexible plastic. 12 in. size fits standard tips and couplers. Also perfect for melting Candy Melts®† in the microwave. Instructions included.

2104-358 Pk./12
2104-1358 Pk./24
2104-1273 Pk./50
2104-1249 Pk./100
† Brand confectionery coating.

Rosewood Spatulas

Quality rosewood handle spatulas have been favorites for years. They have strong, flexible stainless steel blades and sturdy handles.

Straight Blade
11 in.; 6 in. blade.
409-7695
8 in.; 4^1/4 in. blade.
409-6044

Angled Blade
12 in.; 6^1/4 in. blade.
409-135
8 in.; 4^1/2 in. blade.
409-739

Tapered Blade
8 in.; 4 in. blade.
409-518

Comfort Grip™ Spatulas

Decorate with greater comfort, more control and less fatigue, thanks to contoured handle with finger pad. Flexible stainless steel blade is perfect thickness for gliding over icing.

Straight Blade
15 in.; 10^1/8 in. blade.
409-6030
11 in.; 6 in. blade.
409-6018
9 in.; 4^1/2 in. blade.
409-6006

Angled Blade
15 in.; 9^7/8 in. blade.
409-6036
13 in.; 7^3/4 in. blade.
409-6024
9 in.; 4^1/2 in. blade.
409-6012

Tapered Blade
9 in.; 4 in. blade.
409-6003

Cake Boards

Strong corrugated cardboard for strength and stability

Circles

6 in. 2104-64 Pk./10
8 in. 2104-80 Pk./12
10 in. 2104-102 Pk./12
12 in. 2104-129 Pk./8
14 in. 2104-145 Pk./6
16 in. 2104-160 Pk./6

Rectangles

10 x 14 in. 2104-554 Pk./6
13 x 19 in. 2104-552 Pk./6

Cutter/Embosser

Three detachable wheels—straight, wavy and ridged—for cutting and for embossing patterns on fondant. Light, easy-rolling design cuts at the perfect angle. Comfortable handle also stores wheels.

1907-1206

Silicone Baking Mats

Great for cookies—just place on your cookie sheet, roll and cut dough, then bake. Silicone ensures easy release of cookies without spraying or greasing the pan. Heat resistant to 500°F; stain and odor resistant.

10 x 15 in. 2105-4808
11 x 17 in. 2105-4809

Fondant Ribbon Cutter/Embosser Set

This easy-to-use tool is the perfect way to add beautiful textured fondant ribbons, stripes and bows to your cupcakes. Complete set includes: 8 embossing wheels: (4 striped, 4 beaded); 9 spacers (one ^{1}/3 in., two each ^{1}/4, ^{1}/2, ^{3}/4 and 1 in. wide); 9 cutting wheels (3 straight, 3 wavy, 3 zigzag); roller handle with detachable core; assembly hardware.

1907-1203 Set/26

Embossing Wheels   Spacers   Cutting Wheels
4 Beaded 4 Striped   1" ^{3}/4" ^{1}/2" ^{1}/3" ^{1}/4"   3 Straight 3 Zigzag 3 Wavy

Fondant Shaping Foam

Thick and thin squares are the ideal soft surface for shaping flowers, leaves and other fondant or gum paste cutouts. Use the thin square for thinning petal edges with a ball tool, carving vein lines on leaves and making ruffled fondant strips. Use the thick square for cupping flower centers.
Thin: 4 x 4 x ^{1}/8 in. Thick: 4 x 4 x 1 in.

1907-9704 Set/2

Confectionery Tool Set

Invaluable tools for shaping and imprinting, helping you achieve lifelike fondant or gum paste flowers. Ideal for marking patterns in fondant cakes, shaping marzipan fruits. Includes plastic Dogbone, Umbrella, Shell, Ball and Veining tools.

1907-1000 Set/5

Flower Former Set

Dry fondant or icing leaves and flowers in a convex or concave shape. Three each of 1^1/2, 2 and 2^1/2 in. wide holders, all 11 in. long.

417-9500 Set/9

Roll & Cut Mat

For precise measuring, rolling and cutting of fondant or dough. Pre-marked circles for exact sizing. Square grid helps you cut precise strips. Non-stick surface for easy release. 20 in. square with circles from 3 in. to 19 in. diameter.

409-412

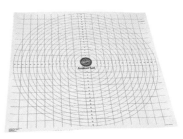

Candy Melts® and Molds

Candy Melts®†
Versatile, creamy, easy-to-melt wafers are ideal for all your candy making—molding, dipping or coating. Their delicious taste can be varied by adding our Candy Flavors. Light and Dark Cocoa are all natural, cocoa flavor; colors are artificially vanilla flavored. 14 oz. bag. Certified Kosher.

† Brand confectionery coating.

Dark Cocoa
1911-358

Light Cocoa
1911-544

Yellow
1911-463

Orange
1911-1631

Blue
1911-448

Red
1911-499

Green
1911-405

White
1911-498

Primary Candy Color Set
Concentrated oil-based colors blend easily with Candy Melts®. Includes Yellow, Orange, Red and Blue in .25 oz. jars. Certified Kosher.

1913-1299 Set/4

Garden Candy Color Set
Create pretty pastel colors! Concentrated oil-based colors blend easily with Candy Melts®. Includes Pink, Green, Violet and Black in .25 oz. jars. Certified Kosher.

1913-1298 Set/4

Candy Melting Plate
Microwave-melt up to 11 Candy Melts® colors at one time with less mess! Plastic with non-slip grip edge. Includes decorating brush.

1904-8016

Numerals
10 designs, 10 cavities.

2115-1564

Deep Heart Truffles
1 design, 7 cavities.

2117-100

Smiley Face Lollipop
1 design, 9 cavities.

2115-1715

Lollipop Sticks
Sturdy paper sticks in 4 sizes. Not for oven use.

4 in.
1912-1006 Pk./50
6 in.
1912-1007 Pk./35
8 in.
1912-9320 Pk./25
11³/4 in.
1912-1212 Pk./20

Candles, Favor Accents & Cake Toppers

Assorted Celebration Candles
Classic spirals in attractive two-tones. 2¹/2 in. high.

2811-215 Pk./24

Chunky Candles
Bigger and bolder designs in 4 colors. Approx. 3¹/4 in. high.

Smiley Stars
2811-6325 Pk./4

Smiley Flames
2811-6326 Pk./4

Shower Rattles Favor Accents
Pink, lavender, blue, yellow, mint green. 3³/4 in. high.

1103-29 Pk./6

Small Derby Clowns Pick Set
2 in. high with pick.

2113-2759 Set/6

Add-A-Message Fun Pix®
Serve party cupcakes in an exciting new way—clip on messages, pictures and more with these colorful picks. Great for place markers, fun sayings and more. 3 in. high.

2113-7611 Pk./12

Keeping In Touch With Wilton

There's always something new at Wilton! Fun decorating courses that will help your decorating skills soar. Exciting cake designs to challenge you. Great new decorating products to try. Helpful hints to make your decorating more efficient and successful. Here's how you can keep up to date with what's happening at Wilton.

Decorating Classes

Do you want to learn more about cake decorating, with the personal guidance of a Wilton instructor? Wilton has two ways to help you.

The Wilton School of Cake Decorating and Confectionery Art is the home of the world's most popular cake decorating system—The Wilton Method. For more than 75 years, thousands of students from around the world have learned to decorate cakes using The Wilton Method. In 1929, Dewey McKinley Wilton taught the first small classes in his Chicago home. Today, The Wilton School teaches more people to decorate than any school in the world. As the school has grown, some techniques have been refined and there are more classes to choose from—but the main philosophies of the Wilton Method have remained.

The Wilton School occupies a state-of-the-art facility in Darien, Illinois. More than 120 courses are offered each year, including The Master Course, a 2-week class that provides individualized instruction in everything from borders and flowers to constructing a tiered wedding cake. Other courses focus on specific subjects, such as Lambeth and Cakes for Catering. Courses in Gum Paste and Chocolate Artistry feature personal instruction from well-known experts.

For more information or to enroll, write to:
Wilton School of Cake Decorating and Confectionery Art
2240 West 75th Street, Woodridge, IL 60517
Attn: School Coordinator

Or visit: www.school.wilton.com
Or call: 800-772-7111, ext. 2888, for a free brochure and schedule.

Wilton Method Class Programs are the convenient way to learn to decorate, close to your home. Wilton Method Classes are easy and fun for everyone. You can learn the fundamentals of cake decorating with a Wilton-trained teacher in just four 2-hour classes. When the course is over, you'll know how to decorate star and shell birthday cakes or floral anniversary cakes like a pro. Everyone has a good time—it's a great place for new decorators to discover their talent. Since 1974, hundreds of thousands have enjoyed these courses.

Special Project Classes are also available in subjects like candy-making, gingerbread, fondant, cookie blossoms and more.

Find classes near you!
In U.S.A., call 800-942-8881 or visit www.wilton.com
In Canada, call 416-679-0790, ext. 200, or email classprograms@wilton.ca
In Mexico, visit www.wiltonmexico.com

Wilton Products

Visit a Wilton Dealer near you. Your local Wilton Dealer is the best place to see the great variety of cake decorating products made by Wilton. If you are new to decorating, it's a good idea to see these products in person; if you are an experienced decorator, you'll want to visit your Wilton Dealer regularly to have the supplies you need on hand. From bakeware and icing supplies to candles and publications, most Wilton retailers carry a good stock of items needed for decorating. Remember, the selection of products changes with each season, so if you want to decorate cakes in time for upcoming holidays, visit often to stock up on current pans, colors and toppers.

Order on-line, by phone or by mail. You can also place orders 24 hours a day at our website, www.wilton.com. Shopping on-line is fast, easy and secure. Or, you can place an order by phone at 800-794-5866 (7WILTON) or by mail, using the Order Form in the Wilton Yearbook of Cake Decorating.

Wilton On The Web

www.wilton.com is the place to find Wilton decorating information on-line. It's filled with great decorating ideas and delicious recipes, updated regularly to fit the season. You'll also find helpful hints, answers to common decorating questions and easy shopping for great Wilton products.

www.cupcakefun.com is the ultimate cupcake website! Go here for essential baking tips, unique and delicious recipes, and creative ways to serve, along with exciting new decorating ideas for all occasions. Plus, the most complete cupcake product selection anywhere!

Wilton Publications

We never run out of decorating ideas! Each year, Wilton publishes more new idea books based on Wilton Method techniques. When you're planning a specific occasion, Wilton books are a fantastic source of decorating inspiration.

The Wilton Yearbook of Cake Decorating is our annual showcase of the latest ideas in decorating. Each edition is packed with all-new cake ideas, instructions and products—it's the best place to find out what's new at Wilton. Cakes for every occasion throughout the year are here: holidays, graduations, birthdays, weddings and more. If you are looking for a new cake to test your decorating skills, you can't beat the Yearbook.

Wilton also regularly publishes special interest decorating books, including books on wedding and holiday decorating, candy-making, home entertaining and food gifting. Look for them wherever Wilton products are sold.